D1565687

THE
STRATEGIC
ETF INVESTOR

Books by Scott Paul Frush

All About Exchange-Traded Funds

Commodities Demystified

Hedge Funds Demystified

Optimal Investing

Understanding Hedge Funds

Understanding Asset Allocation

THE STRATEGIC ETF INVESTOR

HOW TO MAKE MONEY WITH EXCHANGE-TRADED FUNDS

SCOTT PAUL FRUSH, CFA, CFP

New York   Chicago   San Francisco   Lisbon   London
Madrid   Mexico City   New Delhi   San Juan
Seoul   Singapore   Sydney   Toronto

1 2 3 4 5 6 7 8 9 0   DOC/DOC   1 8 7 6 5 4 3 2

ISBN: 978–0–07–179019–2
MHID: 0–07–179019–5

e-ISBN: 978–0–07–179020–8
e-MHID: 0–07–179020–9

This publication is designed to provide accurate and authoritative information in regard to the subject matter covered. It is sold with the understanding that neither the author nor the publisher is engaged in rendering legal, accounting, or other professional service. If legal advice or other expert assistance is required, the services of a competent professional person should be sought.

—*From a Declaration of Principles Jointly Adopted by a Committee of the American Bar Association and a Committee of Publishers and Associations*

McGraw-Hill books are available at special quantity discounts to use as premiums and sales promotions, or for use in corporate training programs. To contact a representative, please e-mail us at bulksales@mcgraw-hill.com.

This book is printed on acid-free paper.

Contents

Acknowledgments

There are a number of excellent people I would like to thank for their generous assistance with various concepts and parts of this book. Thank you to Michael Cafiero of Knight Trading, Scott Krase of ProFunds, Richard Ranck of Invesco PowerShares, Siddharth Jain of KBR, Jason Smull and Rebecca O'Kusky of Vanguard, Jay Gragnani of Dorsey, Wright & Associates, and Craig Lazzara of S&P Indices for your valuable insights on the complex intra workings of the index and ETF creation process, order execution tips, and tax treatment nuances.

Thank you to my past and present editors, Morgan Ertel and Mary Glenn, for helping make this—my sixth book with McGraw-Hill—not only possible but also truly rewarding for me. Also to Scott Kurtz for facilitating such an efficient editing and refining process. For their input—even in the face of exceptionally busy work and personal schedules—I express my gratitude to James Sands, David Bloink, and my wife, Christina.

Scott Paul Frush

Introduction

The guiding principle of this book is to arm investors with the knowledge and tools necessary to engineer and sustain portfolios by using exchange-traded funds (ETFs) as their backbone investments. If you are looking for a book on how to day trade or follow the trends on ETFs to make millions overnight, then stop reading now, as this is not the book for you. However, if you are the type of investor who recognizes that millions of dollars cannot be made overnight using a revolutionary type of wealth-without-risk gimmick, then continue to read on. You'll find the structure of this book to highlight both the concepts of ETFs from a nuts-and-bolts perspective to the full use and application of ETFs to build a winning investment portfolio from a strategic long-term approach.

As you will read throughout the book, the use of the label "ETFs" is not completely accurate and appropriate to describe all exchange-traded portfolios (ETPs), which is a more suitable label from a hierarchical perspective. Nonetheless, given the widespread acceptance and generic use of the label "ETFs," this book will defer to ETFs rather than ETPs when there is no practical reason to distinguish between the two terms. In addition, this book will emphasize passively managed ETFs but does provide detailed information on actively managed ETFs when comparisons and contrasts are appropriately needed.

BEFORE GETTING STARTED

Time and time again I encourage people to manage their portfolio before it manages them. The effort always begins with you—never give up control and oversight carte blanche to someone else even if you are working with a trusted and capable investment professional. When it comes to your investments, you really have two options: accomplish those tasks that will help you manage your portfolio with success or simply forgo them and let your portfolio manage you, for better or worse. Since you are already reading this book, you have demonstrated your ability and willingness to be proactive about managing your portfolio. Consider this book an invaluable tool to help you with this endeavor.

WHAT YOU WILL NOT FIND IN THIS BOOK

The Strategic ETF Investor presents the basics of ETFs and how best to use that knowledge to engineer and sustain your own winning ETF portfolio. Although a good deal of technical information on ETFs is included in this book, my aim has never been to turn off a reader by presenting highly complex topics so that we lose sight of the big picture. There are a couple of books in the marketplace tailored to highly sophisticated investors and portfolio managers that can offer more granularity on the high-level mathematics and complex details of ETFs. The aim of this book is to educate the reader on what's important about ETFs, why they are so beneficial to your investing plan, and how to employ them for the best long-term results.

WHAT IS A STRATEGIC ETF INVESTOR?

From a broad perspective, there are two general types of investors—tactical investors and strategic investors. Tactical investors believe they have the knowledge, skill set, time, and resources to outperform the market on a consistent net long-term basis. This type of investor employs trend following, momentum, and quick hits in an attempt to beat the market.

Throughout this book—and the previous other books I have written—I advocate for and advise investors to rethink their strategy if they believe momentum and trend-following strategies work in all markets and under all conditions to make more-than-deserved performance. For the vast majority of investors, employing a strategic investment strategy is by far the best strategy to employ to generate long-term performance required to achieve financial needs and goals. Strategic investing is not a buy-and-hold investment approach—or worse yet, a buy-and-forget one. Instead, it is grounded in the concepts of optimal asset allocation together with strict rebalancing and smart portfolio construction.

The following are a few of the defining traits of a successful strategic investor:

- **Actionable:** A strategic investor is highly engaged with his or her ETF portfolio and takes action whenever and wherever there is a need. That can be as simple as reviewing monthly account statements to keep tabs on how the portfolio is performing to more complex tasks such as quarterly rebalancing or reallocating.
- **Committed:** A strategic investor understands that to achieve long-term investment success, he must be committed to his investment plan and execute the plan as directed. He knows that his investment plan can—and most likely will—change over time, and he is ready, willing, and able to make the necessary management and portfolio revisions where and when appropriate.
- **Long-term-focused:** A strategic investor recognizes that true investment performance is achieved over the long term and therefore does not attempt to time the market and make short-term bets. She understands that playing the market and gambling in the market are not consistent, practical, and predictable moneymaking strategies.
- **Prudent**: A strategic investor makes decisions as objectively and without emotion as possible. He understands that

emotions can get the best of anyone and therefore sabotage
a solid long-term plan and force behavioral blunders—
such as using blinders or following the crowd—that smart
objective investors avoid at all costs.

- **Able to set goals:** A strategic investor realizes that you
cannot hit a target you are not aiming for. As a result, she
will identify and work to achieve specific goals (e.g., to
contribute 10 percent of net compensation to a trust account
or to generate at least 50 percent of bond interest from tax-
exempt municipal bonds). Little is left to chance.

- **Knowledgeable:** A strategic investor understands not
only the market and his portfolio but also how the
two work together to achieve a long-term investment
plan. He is proactive in learning and understanding
new ETFs, tips, and market dynamics when faced with
something new.

- **Cautious:** A strategic investor realizes that investing
requires a steady and steadfast demeanor for true long-
term performance. She knows that behavioral blunders
can occur at any time and anywhere to undo everything
she has worked so hard and smartly to accomplish, so she
works to avoid them.

- **Familiar:** A strategic investor is familiar with not only
ETFs and how they trade but also with how ETFs fit into
an overall comprehensive ETF portfolio. He recognizes
that investing in something unfamiliar is not especially
smart and can create pitfalls and challenges over time
that can negatively impact his plan and long-term
performance.

- **Portfolio-minded:** A strategic investor understands
that a portfolio behaves in a much different way from its
constituent holdings. Furthermore, she believes in the
expression "garbage in, garbage out" and thereby strives
to construct the best portfolio from the outset.

- **Tax and expense conscious:** A strategic investor understands that it's the net return that matters, not the gross return before taxes, fees, and expenses. He engineers portfolios with this in mind to maximize portfolio value over time.
- **Hands-on:** A strategic investor does not turn a blind eye to what needs to be done. She is proactive with self-investing her portfolio or working with an investment professional to manage the portfolio as planned.

ABBREVIATED HISTORY OF ETFs

The first officially recognized stock market was formed in Amsterdam in the early seventeenth century, and the first commodity exchange—as rudimentary as it now seems—was established in the early eighteenth century in Osaka, Japan. The first mutual fund in the United States was opened during the Roaring Twenties, and the first hedge fund was introduced not long after that. In contrast, ETFs are a relatively new investing instrument that continues to gain new investors and more assets under management each year. Believe it or not, there is modest debate on what constituted the first ETF. Before there was the first ETF as we know it, there were baskets of Standard and Poor's 500 (S&P 500) stocks traded by institutions during the 1970s and a synthetic S&P 500 proxy introduced in 1989 called a "Cash Index Participation (CIP)." The late 1980s also saw the launch of ETPs called "Toronto Index Participation Shares (TIPS)" to track the top 35 stocks on the Toronto Stock Exchange (the TSE 35). The 1993 introduction of the S&P Depository Receipts Trust Series 1, otherwise known as SDPRs or "Spiders" ETF under the trading symbol SPY by the American Stock Exchange and State Street Global Advisors is hailed as the first exchange-traded fund in the United States. However, most experts agree that the aforementioned TIPS ushered in the first real version of the ETF that we know today.

Year	Milestone Event
1989	CIPs and IPSs become the first exchange-traded portfolios introduced
1989	TIPS, the first ETF, is launched by the Toronto Stock Exchange
1990	The SEC issues Release No. 17809 permitting a "SuperTrust"
1993	SPDRs S&P 500 (SPY) becomes the first U.S.-based ETF
1995	Rydex introduces the first currency ETF, the Euro Currency Trust
1996	WEBS become the first ETFs based on a single-country basket
1996	WEBS become the first ETFs to use the investment company structure
1996	Country Baskets become the first ETFs to close
1996	Deutsche Bank launches the first commodity ETF—DB Commodity Index Fund
2000	First mass launch of ETFs with 90 new funds launched in the U.S. in one year
2008	Bear Stearns launches the first actively managed ETF but closes it the same year
2010	The number of U.S. ETFs crosses the 1,000 mark
2010	Various brokerage firms begin offering commission-free trading on select ETFs
2010	U.S. ETF assets surpass $1 trillion on December 16

Figure I-1 **Top Milestones in ETF History**

Ever since the launch of SPY, ETFs have grown by leaps and bounds and are becoming the go-to investment for smart and experienced investors who recognize and understand the significant benefits of using them. According to research from investment manager BlackRock, at the end of 2011 there were 1,370 ETFs (technically ETPs) in the United States with combined assets of $1.06 trillion. For a quick overview of top milestones in the brief history of ETFs, see Figure I-1. For a more detailed discussion of both the growth in assets under management and the development in the number, type, and generation of ETFs coming to the marketplace, see Chapter 1.

A REVIEW OF THE CHAPTERS

The Strategic ETF Investor is divided into 11 chapters plus 3 appendixes. The first chapter of the book provides a solid grounding in the nuts and bolts of ETFs from a cursory perspective. Chapter 2 builds on the information presented in Chapter 1 by drilling down a little deeper to cover the defining attributes of ETFs as well as the indexes ETFs attempt to track. The different types of ETFs—from equity ETFs to sector ETFs and fixed-income ETFs to real asset

ETFs—are presented in Chapter 3. Chapter 4 begins the transition of taking the information about ETFs from concept and theory to personal application to an investment portfolio. This chapter highlights what I consider to be the characteristics that, when combined, create the *perfect* ETF portfolio. Chapter 5 takes a look at the important trade-off between risk and return and how investors need to have a true understanding of this critical relationship. Chapter 6 provides insights into the process, inputs, tools, and strategies that a do-it-yourself investor needs to know when designing, building, and managing an ETF portfolio. The next chapter discusses a number of the important criteria that should be evaluated and compared when picking ETFs to build out a previously established asset allocation. Chapter 8 is for the investors who seek the help of investment professionals instead of attempting to do everything themselves. This chapter will help with sourcing, vetting, and working with an investment professional. To help readers understand how to envision the end result with the designing of portfolios, model ETF portfolios covering various scenarios are presented in Chapter 9. Chapter 10 takes readers into the tax treatment twists of ETFs by type. This is an important chapter for investors with taxable accounts. The last chapter provides a number of keys that can help you achieve success with ETF investing. Finally, the three appendixes provide a resource section, a risk profile questionnaire for establishing your asset allocation, and a glossary of ETF terms for quick and easy reference.

CHAPTER 1

Overview of Exchange-Traded Funds

A fall 2011 research study conducted by Charles Schwab found that approximately 25 percent of survey respondents do not fully understand the cost structure of an exchange-traded fund (ETF) or how to properly employ ETFs as part of an overall effective portfolio strategy. Furthermore, another 46 percent of respondents describe themselves as "ETF novices" while only 8 percent consider themselves experts. If you're not in the 8 percent group of so-called experts, then you are in good company and certainly in the majority. Nonetheless, there are a lot of people who need help learning more about ETFs and how best to utilize them. Let's get started right away with resolving this knowledge gap.

Exchange-traded funds have grown by over 1,000 percent during the 10-year period of 2001 to 2010. At the beginning of 2001, ETFs had combined assets under management (AUM) of approximately $70 billion with nearly 90 funds available in the U.S. marketplace. Fast-forward 10 years to the end of 2010 and AUM have ballooned to over $1 trillion with nearly 1,100 ETFs available in the marketplace. This is extraordinary growth that few ever predicted when the first ETFs were envisioned and launched only decades earlier. (See Figure 1-1 for a list of the 10 most actively traded U.S. ETFs.)

Rank	ETF	Symbol	Volume*
1	SPDR S&P 500	SPY	263,979,875
2	Financial Select Sector SPDR	XLF	114,907,992
3	iShares Russell 2000 Index	IWM	76,650,320
4	iShares MSCI Emerging Markets Index	EEM	74,318,664
5	PowerShares QQQ	QQQ	70,680,820
6	ProShares UltraShort S&P500	SDS	42,453,512
7	Direxion Daily Small Cap Bear 3X Shares	TZA	31,315,000
8	Direxion Daily Small Cap Bull 3X Shares	TNA	30,284,195
9	Vanguard Emerging Markets	VWO	27,754,342
10	iShares FTSE China 25 Index	FXI	26,703,662

*Average daily trading volume over the previous three month period.

Figure 1-1 **Most Actively Traded U.S. ETFs**

ETFs are a relatively recent innovation, but they have become increasingly popular with casual, sophisticated, and institutional investors alike. ETFs offer shareholders, including those of moderate means, an opportunity to invest in a highly diversified, tax-efficient, and cost-effective basket of securities, such as common stocks, preferred stocks, bonds, real estate investment trusts (REITs), and commodities.

ETFs are not investment strategies; they are the basic structure, wrapper, or basket that contains the underlying securities. It is how the securities are managed that dictates an investment strategy or strategies. The same can be said for mutual funds and hedge funds, for that matter. However, each of the aforementioned investment structures offers unique features and characteristics not available—either partially or fully—in the other investment structures. To use an analogy, think of ETFs as a car in which the driver is the ETF provider, the passengers are the shareholders, the engine is the underlying securities, and the road map is the tracking index. A car only drives to where the driver steers it (i.e., the strategy). Cars do not drive themselves. However, not all cars are created the same. Some are faster than others, some are safer than others, some come with more conveniences, some hold more passengers, and some are considered more prestigious. Consequently, some types of investment structures (e.g., ETFs, mutual funds, and hedge funds) make more sense for one strategy or shareholder but not for others.

When ETFs were initially created, they were designed to track market indexes much like the index mutual funds of the day. However, since 2008, when the first actively managed ETF was launched, many of the new ETFs have been designed to follow proprietary customized indexes. This essentially means that these ETFs are tossing aside the traditional index philosophy and incorporating active-management methodologies, all with the intent to outperform the market rather than generate market returns. Many ETF providers that emphasize active management claim their strategies—and therefore their ETFs—are better than all other ETFs in the marketplace. Perhaps the providers will even boast stellar performance to justify their claim. Smart investors know there is no Holy Grail of investing. Most money managers do not outperform their respective benchmarks in any given year, and those that do cannot outperform consistently over time. There will always be money managers who outperform and those who underperform. It's simple mathematics and the law of large numbers. However, where ETFs do add to the bottom line is in their unique structure that affords them favorable cost savings—namely, taxes, expenses, and trading efficiencies. These factors alone give ETFs built-in advantages and shareholders financial benefits and incentives.

WHAT IS AN EXCHANGE-TRADED FUND?

An ETF is an investment company organized under either the Securities Act of 1933 or the Investment Company Act of 1940 that offers shareholders a proportionate share in a portfolio of stocks, bonds, commodities, or other securities. From one perspective, ETFs can be considered a cross between common stocks and mutual funds whereby an ETF trades intraday on a stock exchange at continuously market-determined prices like common stocks and holds a diversified portfolio of securities like a traditional mutual fund. Mutual funds are "forward priced," meaning they can only be purchased and sold at the end of the trading session, whereas ETFs can be traded at any time the market is open for business. Additionally,

ETFs offer stocklike tradability features such as selling short, purchasing via margin, and executing trades using market, limit, stop loss, and other discretionary order types.

One of the most important differences between ETFs and mutual funds is the price at which a shareholder can purchase or sell the fund. Mutual funds are transacted at marked-to-market net asset value (NAV), while ETFs are transacted at market-determined prices, which can differ from NAV. Although the market price for an ETF reflects the market values of the underlying securities, the market price on the fund level is also dictated by simple shareholder supply and demand. Thus, premiums or discounts to NAV can occur. Closed-end funds are much like ETFs in that closed-end funds trade on exchanges and hold pools of securities. However, closed-end funds trade with sometimes significant premiums or more typically discounts to NAV— sometimes as high as 30 percent.

Two features of an ETF's structure ensure that market prices approximate NAV. The first is transparency of holdings. When market participants know an ETF's holdings, they are far less likely to buy or sell at prices that deviate from the aggregate market value— called intraday indicative value (IIV)—associated with the holdings. Second, large institutional investors called authorized participants (APs) are contractually involved to buy or sell ETF shares in a continuous risk-free arbitrage-like manner until the spread between the market price and NAV is negligible. Shareholders benefit from this arrangement as the ETF share price is aligned with its NAV, and APs benefit by making a small profit in the process.

As previously mentioned, ETFs are designed to track either market indexes or proprietary custom indexes. The decision about which index to track is up to the ETF provider. Before an ETF can be listed on an organized stock exchange, such as the NYSE Arca (which we will simply refer to as NYSE throughout this book), an ETF provider must receive approval from an appropriate legal entity. In the United States, approximately 90 percent of ETFs are approved and regulated by the Securities and Exchange Commission (SEC) and the remaining

No.	ETF	Symbol	Market Share	Assets ($B)
1	SPDR S&P 500	SPY	8.2%	$92.7
2	SPDR Gold Shares	GLD	6.9%	$71.2
3	Vanguard MSCI Emerging Markets	VWO	4.2%	$43.9
4	iShares MSCI EAFE Index	EFA	3.5%	$36.3
5	iShares MSCI Emerging Markets	EEM	3.2%	$33.1
6	iShares S&P 500 Index	IVV	2.4%	$25.8
7	PowerShares QQQ	QQQ	2.3%	$24.8
8	iShares Barclays TIPS Bond	TIP	2.1%	$21.8
9	Vanguard Total Stock Market ETF	VTI	1.8%	$19.3
10	iShares iBoxx $ Inv Grade Corp Bond	LQD	1.5%	$16.5

Figure 1-2 **Top 10 Largest U.S. ETFs**

10 percent by the Commodities Futures Trading Commission (CFTC). (See Figure 1-2 for a list of the top 10 largest U.S. ETFs.)

How ETFs Operate

Exchange-traded funds originate with ETF providers, such as Vanguard or PowerShares, which select an ETF's tracking index, establish the basket of securities underlying the ETF, and decide how many shares to offer to the investing marketplace. For instance, when an ETF provider selects an appropriate tracking index, that provider contracts with an AP to obtain the predetermined holdings that make up the basket of securities and to deposit them with the provider. In turn, the provider delivers to the AP what is called a "creation unit" typically representing between 50,000 and 100,000 ETF shares. APs can either hold the ETF shares or sell all or part of them on the open market, which are then purchased by you and me. Chapter 2 provides greater detail of this creation and redemption process.

As a result of the creation and redemption process, shareholders technically do not transact directly with an ETF provider—which is in contrast to mutual funds—and instead transact with APs. The SEC has mandated that ETF providers disclose this material fact in all their prospectuses and other client-approved written materials, such as advertisements.

Major Categories of ETFs

There are six major categories of ETFs available for shareholders to purchase and sell. These ETFs track a number of traditional market indexes in the United States and abroad as well as custom indexes created by ETF providers to employ proprietary investing strategies. These are the six major categories of ETFs:

1. **Broad-based ETFs:** These ETFs track indexes based on both size (large caps, mid caps, and small caps) and style (growth, value, and blend). Examples of these include the SPDR (Spider) S&P 500 ETF and the PowerShares QQQ, which tracks the Nasdaq-100 Index.

2. **Sector and industry ETFs:** These ETFs track indexes that target economic or industry groups such as energy, healthcare, technology, and home builders. Examples include the Financial Select Sector SPDR ETF and the Vanguard Information Technology ETF.

3. **Global ETFs:** These ETFs track indexes that target various countries, geographic regions, and major divisions, such as developing and emerging markets. Examples of these include the Vanguard MSCI Emerging Markets ETF and the iShares MSCI Brazil Index ETF.

4. **Real asset ETFs:** These ETFs track indexes associated with alternative investments such as REITs, commodities, and currencies. Examples of these include the PowerShares DB Commodity Index Tracking ETF and the Vanguard REIT Index ETF.

5. **Fixed-income ETFs:** These ETFs track the expansive bond market including Treasuries, municipals, agencies, and corporates. Examples of these include the Vanguard Total Bond Market ETF and the iShares iBoxx Investment Grade Corporate Bond ETF.

6. **Specialty ETFs:** These ETFs track indexes associated
    with less traditional investment approaches such as
    leveraged and inverse strategies. Examples of these
    include the ProShares Ultra Financials ETF and the
    Direxion Daily Financial Bear 3X Shares ETF.

ETF Expenses

Exchange-traded funds that follow a strict passive-management
strategy typically have very low management fees—generally less
than 30 basis points, or the equivalent of 0.3 percent. For ETFs
that employ a more active management strategy, expenses will
be higher, oftentimes around 60 basis points or more. In addition to management fees, shareholders will need to transact these
shares on an exchange, and that means trading commissions will
be incurred for both purchases and sales. As a result, be mindful
and consider the expenses of these funds prior to building a portfolio of them.

Undivided Interest in ETFs

When a shareholder purchases shares of an ETF, that shareholder
owns an undivided and proportional interest in each of the underlying securities. All outstanding shareholders do not divvy up each
underlying security whereby each takes a few shares of one or two
stocks. Shareholders are owners of each and every security held in
the ETF. Consider an analogy of three people going into business
with one another and buying a car dealership in equal proportion.
Each of the three business owners will own an undivided interest in
the tools in the shop, the buildings on the property, and the cars for
sale on the lot. What doesn't happen is one person gets the tools,
another person the building, and the last person the cars on the lot.
Each owns an undivided interest in all of these and the other assets.
The same goes for ETF shareholders.

ETF REGULATION AND ISSUANCE

Exchange-traded products are regulated by a number of divisions within the Securities and Exchange Commission (SEC) as well as other regulatory entities, such as the Commodity Futures Trading Commission (CFTC). Within the SEC, the Division of Trading and Markets (formerly known as the SEC Division of Market Regulation) is charged with the responsibility of regulating the "exchange-traded" feature of ETPs—including the regulation of all major stock exchanges in the United States. Additionally, the SEC Division of Investment Management is charged with the responsibility of regulating the "portfolio" feature. There is a clear and distinct separation of enforcement and regulatory duties between divisions and entities within and outside of the SEC. For example, the CFTC has jurisdiction over commodity-based exchange-traded portfolios (ETPs), while the SEC Division of Corporate Finance holds jurisdiction over exchange-traded notes (ETNs). The SEC adheres to and enforces rules and regulations based on a number of acts of Congress.

Government Regulation

The two most important and applicable legislative acts impacting the registration, issuance, and ongoing oversight of ETFs—and all other ETPs—are the Securities Act of 1933 and the Investment Company Act of 1940.

Securities Act of 1933

In the aftermath of the stock market crash of 1929, the U.S. Congress enacted the Securities Act of 1933, requiring that any offer or sale of securities using the means and instrumentalities of interstate commerce be registered pursuant to the 1933 act, unless an exemption from registration exists under U.S. law.

The enactment of the 1933 act is considered a milestone event in securities legislation because it was the first major piece of federal legislation to regulate the offer and sale of securities—a task primarily given to the states and regulated under state laws, commonly referred to as blue-sky laws. Unless a security qualifies for an exemption, any security offered or sold to the public in the United States must be registered by filing a registration statement— typically along with a prospectus—with the SEC. The SEC then conducts a thorough screening of the proposed security—a process that can take many months or even years.

Investment Company Act of 1940

To again help restore the public's confidence in the stock market after the 1929 crash, Congress passed the Investment Company Act of 1940 on August 22, 1940. The aim was to enhance regulations of investment companies to protect the interests of the public by setting strict standards of conduct. Many provisions of this act were updated by the Dodd-Frank Act of 2010.

Under this act, investment companies were now required to establish regular reporting procedures for each fund, set minimum standards of fund diversification, and introduce new rules for advertising; the act gave the SEC regulatory oversight. Material facts— including conflicts of interest—were now required to be disclosed to the investing public. Furthermore, the act required investment companies to disclose all material facts concerning their financial health.

Most importantly, the act strictly defined and divided investment companies into three classifications: face-amount certificate companies, unit investment trusts (UITs), and investment management companies. Before 1940 no standard for what an investment company looked like was yet established. Imagine that.

Exemptive Relief

When the Investment Company Act of 1940 was drafted, Congress could not have envisioned the creation of or demand for ETFs some 50-plus years later. As a result, for ETFs to receive approval from the SEC, they need to be granted exemptive relief from a number of rules and regulations associated with the 1940 Act. Let's investigate four of the most pressing needs.

First, ETF providers must be permitted to issue shares redeemable only in large blocks: creation units. Thus, exemptive relief is needed from Section 22d and Rule 22c-1. Second, in-kind purchase and redemption of creation units by authorized participants must be allowed; thus exemptive relief from Sections 17(a) and 17(b) is needed. Third, exemptive relief from Rule 22c-1 is needed to permit trading of shares to occur at prices other than at the net asset value (NAV). Finally, an exemption needs to be granted allowing investment companies to purchase shares of the ETF in excess of current regulations—Section 12(d)(1). Petitioning the SEC to grant the aforementioned exemptions and others is a time-consuming and costly activity. Given the significant growth in ETFs and the need for exemptions, the SEC announced in 2008 a proposal to adopt Rule 6c-11, a regulation change that would automatically grant several exemptions without the need to seek exemptions for each new ETF.

Legal Structures

For most investors, ETFs represent all funds that are listed and traded on an exchange. Unbeknownst to many, ETFs are just one of the many different types of ETPs available. Even the *Wall Street Journal* lists prices for ETFs under the title "Exchange-Traded Portfolios." This is an appropriate move, since many special trusts, limited partnerships, and notes have the same look and feel as an ETF, but they simply do not have many of the same important characteristics. Nonetheless, the use of the term ETF has become engrained in popular culture and is now the preferred title for all ETPs. As mentioned, many ETPs, do not have all—and some have none—of the primary characteristics that define ETFs. Some ETPs are not truly low cost, while others are not tax efficient. For example, consider currency funds, where, by law, gains are taxed as ordinary income—which is typically a higher rate than taxes on capital gains. Still others do not have a creation and redemption process.

The paragraphs that follow provide a brief overview of each legal structure to enable investors to better differentiate each type of ETP.

Closed-End Fund

Closed-end funds (CEFs), like ETFs, are collective investments whereby investors pool their money in one fund that invests in an underlying basket of securities. Figure 1-3 outlines some of the prominent similarities and differences.

Contrary to misconception, closed-end funds are not closed to new investors. But closed-end funds do not issue new shares of the fund once the initial shares are sold to investors. Once that happens, the only way investors can purchase shares is in the secondary market on a stock exchange. This means that prices for closed-end funds are dictated by supply-and-demand forces, much like that of ETFs. However, closed-end funds do not involve authorized participants (APs) and therefore cannot arbitrage away any trading premiums or discounts to NAV. This disadvantage is actually an advantage to some investors, who only invest in closed-end funds and make purchase and sale decisions based solely on the amount of premium or discount and on how that premium or discount is changing over time. Furthermore, some investors seek out closed-end funds that they believe will experience narrowing in the discount to NAV.

For example, suppose an investor purchases a certain closed-end fund for $20 per share when the net asset value is $22. If the discount were to narrow from $2 to $1 per share, then the investor

Characteristic	ETFs	Closed-End Funds
Organization Method	Investment Company Act of 1940	Investment Company Act of 1940
Method of Launch	Seeded and Listed	IPO
Exchange Traded?	Yes	Yes
Number of Outstanding Shares	Changing	Fixed
Stocklike Tradability?	Yes	Yes
Traded at Premiums and Discounts?	No	Yes
Can Be Sold Short?	Yes	Yes
Purchased on Margin?	Yes	Yes
Portfolio Turnover	Low	Low
Source Liquidity from Underlying Holdings?	Yes	No

Figure 1-3 **Differences Between ETFs and Closed-End Funds**

would make $1—even if the value of the underlying securities stayed the same. Most closed-end funds trade with discounts that range from 15 to 25 percent of NAV; given these sizable discounts, closed-end funds are more price volatile than other ETFs. Regardless of the presence of discounts or premiums, closed-end funds offer an alternative way for people to invest their money. If you want to know more about closed-end funds, the Closed-End Fund Association (CEFA), a national trade association of approximately two dozen fund managers, can offer help. Their association's website is www.cefa.com.

Unit Investment Trust

Organized under the Investment Company Act of 1940, the UIT structure was the first legal structure employed to launch ETFs. Today, some of the most well-known ETFs are organized as UITs, including SPDR S&P 500, SPDR Dow Jones Industrial Average "Diamonds," and finally the PowerShares QQQ Trust, which tracks the Nasdaq-100 Index. Unlike the subsequent open-end fund structure, UITs are required to include all securities comprising an index; no sampling or optimization is permitted. ETF providers do not have the discretion as to which securities to include and which to remove; they must include all securities of the tracking index—no less and no more. The only flexibility granted by the SEC is the timing of when to make the fund rebalancing needed to track an index that has recently been reconstituted.

Additional restrictions include the following:

- No more than 25 percent of the assets of the fund can be tied to a company that has a weighting of 5 percent or greater.
- No more than 50 percent of the assets of an ETF can be tied to industry sectors or concentrated holdings.
- No more than 10 percent of the voting stock of any one company can be controlled by the fund.

These restrictions are typically not of concern for most broadly diversified UITs but they can be problematic for funds that target economic sectors or specific country segments. Finally, even though UITs may receive a dividend from an underlying stock, the fund is not permitted to reinvest the money back into shares of the underlying stocks. Instead, the fund must hold dividends in non-interest-bearing escrow accounts until quarter end when the fund distributes the accumulated cash to shareholders. Because the performance of the tracked index includes the immediate reinvestment of dividends, tracking error will occur. This performance penalty is referred to as dividend drag.

Open-End Fund (Regulated Investment Company)

Most newly launched ETFs are organized as open-end funds (and therefore regulated investment companies, or RICs) under the Investment Company Act of 1940. There are five primary reasons for this trend. First and foremost, the RIC structure provides significant flexibility to ETF providers for managing underlying holdings. Gone is the restriction that an ETF must make up each and every security in the tracking index as with the UIT structure. Instead, an RIC can use sampling and optimization to track an index. RICs can also include futures, options, and fixed-income securities as well as common stocks.

Second, in contrast to UITs, RICs are permitted to reinvest—rather than accrue in escrow accounts—dividends by purchasing additional shares of the paying stocks. This eliminates the performance penalty associated with dividend drag that other ETFs may experience.

Third, ETFs organized as RICs are permitted to invest up to 50 percent of their assets in single concentrated positions and 25 percent in any one security, provided the ETFs are registered as nondiversified funds and control no more than 10 percent of any one company's voting stock.

Fourth, the RIC structure also provides for an unusual, but very lucrative, activity: the loaning of underlying securities. When a regulated investment company loans underlying securities, the extra revenue they earn can be used to offset operating expenses and thus charge reduced expense ratios to shareholders. BlackRock, Vanguard, State Street, and other large ETF providers are highly engaged in this activity for this very reason.

Fifth, ETFs organized as RICs give shareholders the right to vote the shares they own. To some shareholders this is extremely important; to others, it's much less so. The leading drawback of the RIC structure results from the inherent flexibility that providers have in managing the fund. As a result, poor decisions and policies on behalf of ETF providers lead to tracking error and therefore potential underperformance of the tracking index.

Grantor Trust

An exchange-traded grantor trust is not an RIC nor a UIT; instead, it is registered under the Securities Act of 1933. Shareholders have voting rights in the underlying companies and can transact shares in round lots of 100. Dividends are not reinvested in the trust and are instead paid immediately to shareholders. The portfolio of stocks under the exchange-traded grantor trust does not change and, as a result, cannot be rebalanced. Over time, this arrangement will ultimately lead to a less diversified portfolio since some of the underlying stocks appreciate in value while others are removed by merger, acquisition, or bankruptcy. Some ETPs organized under the grantor trust structure are commodity linked. Under this arrangement, actual physical commodities are held by the trust and thus constitute the underlying holdings. Three of the most widely recognized ETPs include CurrencyShares, iShares Gold Trust, and iShares Silver Trust.

Holding Company Depository Receipt

A type of grantor trust, a holding company depository receipt (HOLDR) is very much like an ETF from the perspective of investing in a fund where the underlying securities track a certain index or market segment. However, HOLDRs are not actually funds like ETFs. HOLDRs may resemble ETFs, but there are several important dissimilarities.

First, HOLDRs represents a pool of only 20 initial stocks that are held in a grantor trust owned by Merrill Lynch, the brainchild behind the product. Over time, the number of stocks in the trust can fall as the companies are acquired or merge with other companies. No replacements are made to the trust when a company is removed. As mentioned, this will ultimately lead to a less diversified fund, much like the Internet Holding HOLDRs (symbol: HHH) where more than 50 percent of its fund is invested in Yahoo! and eBay with no allocation to Google since the initial public offering (IPO) was issued after the fund creation date.

Second, unlike the UIT structure ETFs, where the voting rights are held by the ETF providers and not by the fund shareholders, HOLDRs provide the unique ability for shareholders to receive proxies and vote directly on issues involving the companies held in the trust, such as voting on the board of directors.

Third, shareholders of HOLDRs are entitled to receive dividends directly from the companies held in the trust. Fourth, shareholders do not pay expense ratios and instead are assessed an annual custody fee per share for cash dividends and distributions. Finally, to invest in HOLDRs, a shareholder must purchase and sell shares in blocks of 100, which is in contrast to ETFs, where trades can be executed with as little as one share. HOLDRs typically cover a narrow market segment, such as Biotech (symbol: BBH) or Broadband (symbol: BDH) HOLDRs.

Exchange-Traded Note

First issued in 2006 by Barclays Bank, exchange-traded notes (ETNs) are debt instruments that track the return of a single currency, commodity, or index. See Figure 1-4 for a comparison of ETFs and ETNs. In contrast to ETFs, ETNs do not hold or represent a pool of underlying securities. Instead, ETNs are senior, unsecured, unsubordinated direct debt of a leading bank and registered under the Securities Act of 1933. Exchange-traded notes employ an arbitrage strategy whereby market prices are closely linked to the intrinsic value of the benchmarks each ETN tracks. Exchange-traded notes are established with 30-year maturities and offer no principal protection. In addition, ETNs do not pay dividends or interest payments, do not offer voting rights to shareholders, and are subject to call provisions at the discretion of the issuer.

The primary drawback or risk of investing in ETNs is the credit risk associated with the issuing bank. If the credit rating of the issuing bank were to be cut, then the value of the ETN might fall even though there would be no change to the tracking index. A bankruptcy by the issuer can lead to a completely worthless investment.

The primary advantage of exchange-traded notes is their favorable tax treatment, whereby positions held for at least one year are taxed as long-term capital gains and thus receive lower tax rates. This is especially important for those investors who hold taxable portfolios and wish to gain exposure to specific sectors of the commodities market. Secondary advantages include stocklike tradability and the opportunity to invest in defined market segments such as grains, sugar, and livestock.

Investors who hold exchange-traded notes have three ways to liquidate their investment:

- Sell the shares in the secondary market as with any other security
- Sell the shares through a weekly redemption program with the issuing bank for cash (only for large shareholders)
- Hold the shares to maturity and receive the market value of the position in cash from the issuing bank

Characteristic	ETFs	ETNs
Ability to Sell Short?	Yes	Yes
Composition of Instrument	Portfolio of Securities	Issuer Credit
Continuous Pricing and Trading Throughout the Day?	Yes	Yes
Distribution of Dividends?	Yes	No
Have a Maturity Date?	No	Yes
Have a Net Asset Value (NAV)?	Yes	No
Marginable?	Yes	Yes
Method of Registration and Regulation	Investment Company Act of 1940	Securities Act of 1933
Purchased Through a Traditional Brokerage Account and IRA?	Yes	Yes
Quantity Available	Significant	Few
Risks to Investment	Market Risk	Market Risk and Issuer Credit Risk
Tax Treatment	Typically similar to stocks where positions held for longer than one year qualify for long-term capital gains treatment	Similar to stocks where positions held for longer than one year qualify for long-term capital gains treatment

Figure 1-4 **Differences Between ETFs and ETNs**

Traded Commodity Pool

One of the most recent innovations with ETPs is the exchange-traded commodity pool—typically organized as Delaware limited partnerships. Traded commodity pools are not registered with or regulated by the SEC under the Investment Company Act of 1940. Instead, traded commodity pools are regulated by the Commodity Futures Trading Commission (CFTC). Exchange-traded funds that hold physical commodity positions are regulated by the SEC under the Securities Act of 1933, however. About 10 percent of all assets held in ETFs are invested in traded commodity pools.

These partnerships or trusts issue units that may be purchased and sold on the New York Stock Exchange. Instead of using stocks or physical commodities for the underlying holdings, the partnership uses commodity futures contracts and other commodity-linked futures, forwards, and swap contracts to gain the targeted exposure it desires. Shareholders become limited partners when they invest in a traded commodity pool, while the general partners (equivalent to ETF providers) oversee the management of the partnership assets. One of the largest general partners is United States Commodity Funds, LLC, who runs the popular United States Oil Fund (symbol: USO) and the United States Natural Gas Fund (symbol: UNG). Similar to other exchange-traded funds, traded commodity pools attempt to generate a return that tracks specific indexes rather than try to outperform them outright.

Traded commodity pools have come under intense scrutiny over the last couple of years, given their inherent drawback when exposed to what is called "contango." Contango is a pricing situation in which futures prices get progressively higher as monthly contract dates get progressively longer. As a result, when a monthly contract is rolled forward, the contract must be purchased at a higher price than that of the previous monthly contract, thus creating negative spreads and hurting performance. Nonetheless, traded commodity pools offer investors an extra option to gain exposure to target commodity classes.

STATE OF THE ETF MARKETPLACE

Increasingly higher demand for ETFs has led many ETF providers to rapidly increase the number of ETFs they make available in the investing marketplace. Until 2008, few ETFs were dissolved, but the financial crisis and market crash caused some providers to liquidate their ETFs because of lack of investor interest and, more importantly, insufficient AuM, the lifeblood of any ETF. Almost 100 ETFs were liquidated in the two-year period of 2008 to 2009, 10 times more than the preceding eight years combined.

The number of U.S. ETFs available in the marketplace has never declined year over year. At the end of 2001, there were

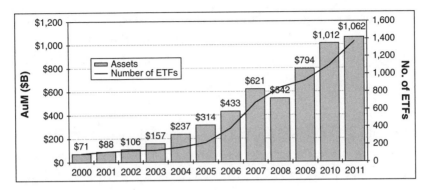

Figure 1-5 **U.S. ETF AuM and Number by Year**

118 ETFs in existence—which sounds bizarre today, given their popularity and incredible reach. But at the end of 2011, there were approximately 1,370 ETFs in existence—an 11-fold increase (see Figure 1-5).
Although the number of ETFs has been increasing slowly each year,
it was during the mid-2000s that they really took off. By the end of
2005, there were about 221 ETFs; two years later the number had
risen to 673, more than tripling the availablity in the marketplace.
Even the abnormal number of closings in 2008 and 2009 was not
enough to stem the tide of new issues when over 200 ETFs were
launched during this two-year period. Once the financial crisis had
peaked and began receding, ETF providers began flooding the market with new funds; the year 2010 alone saw an increase of over
20 percent in the number of available options. One would think this
rate of increase cannot continue, but we may be in for a sustainable
growth for the foreseeable future as presently more than 600 ETFs
are somewhere in the registration process with the SEC.

Assets under Management

At the end of the twentieth century, U.S. ETF assets under management stood at about $70 billion, and two years later they increased
to just a little over $100 billion. From this point on, inflows of assets
began to gain traction, and total AuM hit $600 billion during 2007
just before the beginning of the financial crisis. Although 2008 saw

assets under management fall from the prior year, the level of assets rebounded by the end of 2009 and closed above their 2007 peak. By the end of 2011, total assets under management were over $1 trillion.

Annual Inflows and Outflows

Throughout the 2000s, inflows of assets into U.S. exchange-traded funds were always positive, even during 2008 when market values caused total assets to fall year over year (see Figure 1-6). Coincidently, 2008 witnessed the biggest year for ETF inflows at nearly $180 billion, the same year asset inflows into ETFs surpassed inflows into mutual funds for the first time on an annual basis. The year with the second highest asset inflows was 2007 when nearly $150 billion was invested into ETFs by shareholders. The year with the smallest inflow of assets into ETFs was 2003 at just over $15 billion.

Demand for ETFs

There is no question that the demand for ETFs has increased steadily since their introduction. To meet the increasing demand, ETF providers have launched more funds that have a greater variety of investment objectives and that track lesser-known indexes. During the mid-1990s, ETF providers began launching international equity ETFs, with significant traction gained in these funds

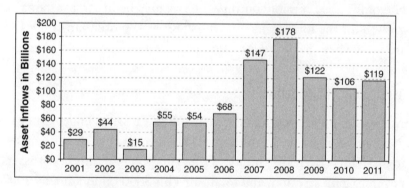

Figure 1-6 **ETF Annual Inflows**

No.	ETF	Symbol	Inflows ($B)
1	Vanguard MSCI Emerging Markets	VWO	$7.8
2	SPDR S&P 500	SPY	$6.6
3	iShares MSCI EAFE Index	EFA	$5.4
4	Vanguard Total Bond Market	BND	$5.2
5	Vanguard Dividend Appreciation	VIG	$4.1
6	Market Vectors Agribusiness	MOO	$3.7
7	iShares iBoxx $ High Yield Corporate Bond	HYG	$3.5
8	iShares iBoxx $ Inv Grade Corp Bond	LQD	$3.3
9	PowerShares QQQ	QQQ	$3.2
10	SPDR Select Sector Utilities	XLU	$3.1

Figure 1-7 **Top 10 ETFs with Highest Full-Year 2011 Inflows**

in the early to mid-2000s. Toward the end of the past decade, emerging markets ETFs led the way with nearly 15 percent of all AuM invested, making it the second largest category of ETFs behind large-cap domestic ETFs (see Figure 1-7 for a list of the top 10 ETFs with the highest full-year 2011 inflows). The third most popular category is bond and hybrid ETFs, with developed international ETFs not too far behind. One of the fastest-growing segments is commodity-linked ETFs. Approximately two-thirds of commodity-linked ETF assets track precious metals via both the spot and futures markets. Consumer and utility ETFs have two of the lowest assets under management of all commodity and sector funds.

Finally, there are over 20 ETF funds of funds (i.e., ETFs that hold and invest primarily in shares of other ETFs), with approximately $1 billion of AuM. This category should continue to grow exponentially as ETFs migrate into 401(k) and 403(b) retirement plan platforms.

ETF PLAYERS AND PARTICIPANTS

The following section provides a cursory review of the major players and participants involved in varying degrees in the ETF marketplace. The list is arranged according to approximately where the participant falls in the timeline from blueprint of an ETF to eventual investment.

- **ETF providers:** The investment companies that design, introduce, and oversee each ETF in existence today. Examples include Vanguard, BlackRock (iShares), State Street Global Advisors (SPDRs), and Invesco (PowerShares) (see Figure 1-8).
- **Index sponsors:** The companies that create the indexes, such as the S&P 500, that ETFs attempt to track. Some examples are Standard & Poor's, Dow Jones Indexes, Morningstar, and Wilshire Associates.
- **Government "industry" regulators:** Federal, state, industry, and international entities that make and enforce rules to ensure the viability and efficiency of the financial markets, including the ETF marketplace. Some examples are the SEC, the Federal Reserve, the U.S. Treasury Department, and the CFTC.
- **Stock exchanges:** The companies that provide the electronic trading framework, liquidity, and price discovery where the buying and selling of stocks and ETFs are accomplished. Examples include the New York Stock Exchange, the Nasdaq, and the Toronto Stock Exchange.

Rank	ETF Provider	Assets ($B)	# of ETFs	Market Share
1	BlackRock (iShares)	$ 449.1	246	42.3%
2	StateStreet (SPDRs)	$ 257.1	106	24.2%
3	Vanguard	$ 170.3	64	16.1%
4	Invesco (PowerShares[1])	$ 57.7	129	5.4%
5	Van Eck (Market Vectors)	$ 23.5	43	2.2%
6	ProFunds (ProShares)	$ 23.1	129	2.2%
7	WisdomTree	$ 12.2	47	1.1%
8	Bank of New York Mellon	$ 8.9	6	0.8%
9	Rydex SGI	$ 7.7	37	0.7%
10	Direxion	$ 6.7	55	0.6%

[1]*Includes DB Commodity Services*

Figure 1-8 **Top 10 Largest U.S. ETF Providers**

- **Authorized participants:** Typically, large institutional investors, specialists, market makers, or lead market makers (LMMs) that have signed participant agreements with specific ETF providers to transact directly with providers in a process for share creations and redemptions. Some examples are Deutsche Bank, Goldman Sachs, LaBranche Structured Products, and Société Générale.
- **Lead market makers:** Formerly known as specialists, the companies that are contracted liquidity providers on an exchange with obligations to maintain continuous ETF quotes, provide price discovery, and drive the inside quote a certain percentage of time throughout the day.
- **Distributors:** The companies that not only act as a liaison between the ETF custodian and the APs but also help to facilitate the sale of ETFs to both retail and institutional investors. Some ETFs take on this role themselves through a subsidiary, while others work with an external partner.
- **Custodians:** Specialized financial organizations that are responsible for physically holding, record keeping, and safeguarding financial assets—namely, the underlying securities of an ETF—and serve the traditional role of transfer agent and fund administrator. Some examples include Bank of New York Mellon, BNP Paribas, and Wells Fargo Bank.
- **Broker-dealers:** Either the full-service or discount brokerage houses that facilitate ETF buy and sell orders from everyday shareholders. Examples include TD Ameritrade, Scottrade, Charles Schwab, Merrill Lynch, UBS, and Wells Fargo Advisors.
- **News and research sources:** The companies involved in disseminating news, research, and analysis on ETFs. Some examples are Morningstar, IndexUniverse.com (including its Journal of Indexes), Value Line, ETFGuide.com, ETFTrends.com, and SeekingAlpha.com.

- **Investment professionals:** Both the portfolio managers and investment advisors that either help manage a portfolio of ETFs or provide advice and other financial support to clients and shareholders. Examples of titles include Certified Financial Planner, Chartered Financial Analyst, and Certified Fund Specialist.
- **Shareholders:** The end users of ETFs and final links in the ETF chain. Examples of these include casual retail investors, experienced trading speculators, and institutions of all sizes.

BENCHMARKS AND STRATEGIES THAT ETFS TRACK

The focal point of any exchange-traded fund is the underlying index the ETF tracks. The index serves as a road map for the ETF, and without it an ETF will not reach its intended destination. Moreover, ETFs are benchmarked to an ever-growing universe of indexes— some older and others recently established. These indexes range from fundamental passive benchmarks (e.g., the S&P 500) to custom indexes employing sophisticated quantitative strategies and alternative weighting methods. As a result, understanding the difference among indexes, their intended purpose, and the way they are created is essential to building an ideal ETF portfolio. Not having at least a cursory understanding of the underlying indexes can cause individuals to sabotage their financial plan and doom their portfolio.

Indexes can be classified by general purpose and underlying specific strategy. The investment profession recognizes two basic types of indexes: market indexes and custom indexes. A market index is a traditional and fundamental nuts-and-bolts measure of market value using passive security selection and weightings based on current market capitalization (i.e., the value of a company's outstanding stock calculated by multiplying the market price for a share of stock by the number of common stock shares outstanding). Since they reflect good cross sections of a market, market indexes are tools used to measure and analyze changes in a market segment given changes in each of the underlying holdings. Conversely, a custom index is best described as a strategy, no less and no more. A custom or strategy index is a method for investment selection rather than a tool to measure and analyze overall changes. Since a market index tracks a specific market segment, it represents that particular market and by definition provides beta, or the market return—less tracking error—and market risk as measured by volatility. In contrast, custom indexes do not track a particular or well-defined market segment and thus by definition attempt to generate outperformance, or alpha.

Many newly issued ETFs track custom indexes: themselves strictly strategy based and provide little to no meaningful insights into the pulse of the market. Custom indexes cannot be used to compare against other indexes, nor can they be used to guide asset allocation policy decisions. Custom indexes provide little relevance for evaluating levels of changes in economic progress and resulting investor confidence. Only market indexes can serve this important role. Custom indexes are designed subjectively, with security selection and security weighting—according to specific rules-based methodologies—of utmost importance.

Comparing custom indexes is like comparing apples and oranges. There is simply no viable connection between them for most indexes. Consequently, there has been only modest research into the benefit that custom indexes bring to investment management. To compound the issue, the Securities and Exchange Commission does not define what indexes should look like or how they should be structured or constructed. This lack of overall direction means investors can sometimes lose sight of what true indexing and passive management are all about. To take advantage of the environment, many providers of actively managed ETFs have aggressively pushed their claim that their indexing methodology is far superior to that of others—especially ETFs using market indexes—and therefore you should invest in their ETFs. Troublesomely, the days of relying on tried-and-true market indexes based on capitalization weights and market representation are now under siege. The growth of custom index ETFs is gaining far more momentum than the growth in ETFs using market indexes.

One of the largest custom index sponsors is actually Standard and Poor's, the manager of the exceptionally well-known and quoted S&P 500 stock index. Custom index sponsors view indexes through a money-generating looking glass, whereas indexes are created using rules-based methodologies and then licensed to ETF providers that create corresponding ETFs and pay continuing royalty fees to the index sponsor. ETF providers will then stake claims that their strategy—based on a custom index—is far superior to "old-fashioned" market indexes. Make no mistake, the investing business is very big money, and any edge is exploited with extreme effort.

Purposes of Indexes

Indexes serve three primary roles. The first and most important is that of a benchmark, whereby a comparison of performance as an asset class can be made against other asset classes, such as the S&P 500 and real estate investment trusts. Here market indexes are used as yardsticks. The second purpose of an index is that of indicator, whereby changes in the index will offer an indication of how well or poorly a particular market segment is doing. Economic research is often conducted using indexes as indicators. The third purpose of an index is that of an investable instrument, whereby investors can gain exposure through the purchase of an ETF (or perhaps mutual fund) that tracks the index. Be aware that not all indexes have ETFs or index mutual funds that track them—thereby rendering them noninvestable.

The CFA Institute, arguably the top industry organization for investment management, provides guidelines on what attributes it believes define best-of-breed indexes. These characteristics include the following:

- **Comprehensive:** Indexes should incorporate all opportunities that are realistically available for investment by all market participants under normal market conditions.
- **Reasonable expenses:** The index should not charge excessive costs, and all expenses should be understood by market participants.

- **Low barriers to entry:** The markets or market segments tracked by an index should not contain significant barriers to entry.
- **Relevant:** The index should be relevant and of interest to market participants for investing purposes.
- **Replicable:** The total returns for an index should be replicable by and readily available to all market participants.
- **Simple and objective:** Indexes should be created, forecasted, and modified according to clear sets of rules governing the inclusion of securities or markets.
- **Stable:** The index should not change composition frequently. When changes are needed, they should be easily understood and very predictable.

Index Creation

Custom indexes are tailored to a specific strategy an ETF provider wants to employ and advertise to investors. The ETF provider may target a particular asset class or sector but may keep the parameters quite broad. Also, the provider may include leverage or design an ETF that moves inversely to a predetermined index. The options are vast and varied. Market indexes, on the other hand, tend to be passively selected, either incorporating all the securities in a particular market segment or using a cross-section sample of the market. The intent is not to design a strategy that will outperform a specific market segment but instead to design an index that captures and replicates the performance of a specific market segment.

Market Capitalization Weighting

When prices for the securities underlying an index change, the index value itself will change. But this calculation is not as straightforward as it might appear. Why? Some companies in an index have larger market capitalizations, meaning they are bigger than some of the others. So the important question is how to weight the companies to provide the best measure of price change on the index level. Market indexes have taken the position that the companies should be capitalization weighted, meaning that larger market capitalization companies exhibit greater influence on the economy and index than do small market capitalization companies. This is not a material issue for indexes that track specific market capitalization segments, such as small caps and mid caps, but it is for indexes that do not segment by size.

There are times when small price movements in large-capitalization securities will influence the index far more than large price movements in small-capitalization securities. As a result, the use of market capitalization-weighted indexes has come under fire from some people who claim this indexing method is trend following and therefore creates an inefficient risk and return trade-off profile. Irrespective of the claims, market capitalization more closely tracks a market, because in reality companies are of various sizes.

Market capitalization can be divided into four types: full cap, free float, capped, and liquidity. Full cap uses the traditional calculation of market capitalization, whereas the free-float type uses a market capitalization based on the amount of shares available for trading to the public. This is an important distinction since many companies have meaningful amounts of stock that are restrictive, such as those tied up by corporate employees. Capped is used to control the impact from one or more companies that dominate the index based on market capitalization. Under this type, the weighting for any one security may be capped at a specific percentage—such as 10 percent. The liquidity type essentially takes the free float to a more stringent level. Here, only the normal trading volume in a particular security is used in the calculation. This helps to alleviate a situation in which a security has a much lower trading volume than other securities with comparable free floats.

The market capitalization-weighted method is not the only method available. A newer methodology, referred to as fundamentally weighted, is making modest inroads with index sponsors. This method weights securities based on company fundamentals such as revenue, dividend rates, earnings, and book value.

Another popular methodology is called equal-weight capitalization, which is primarily used by ETF providers that focus on custom indexes. As the name implies, with this method each security in the index is weighted the same. The benefit of this method is that each security has a proportional influence on the index and eliminates any significant influence from much larger capitalization securities and therefore the market as a whole. The obvious drawback is that these indexes are not truly representative of changes in the underlying securities. For example, an equal capitalization-weighted index comprising only Microsoft (over $250 billion market cap) and JDS Uniphase (under $4 billion market cap) will show a 2 percent return if Microsoft were to gain 1 percent and JDS Uniphase 3 percent in a single trading day. As you can see, the smaller company—JDS Uniphase—influenced the index as much as the substantially larger Microsoft did. Nonetheless, the market capitalization-weighting, fundamentally weighted, and equal capitalization-weighting methods are popular with particular ETF providers and thus will be around for the foreseeable future.

Indexes by Market Segment

In addition to broad-market indexes, there are other indexes that track more defined styles, sectors, and fixed-income segments. Examples include large-cap value, large-cap growth, small-cap value, and small-cap growth. Sectors include, but are not limited to, financials, healthcare, utilities, and technology. Fixed-income segments can be made up of corporate bonds, municipal bonds, mortgage-linked bonds, and Treasuries. There are also international and real assets.

This differentiation is important since broad indexes are essentially the sum of their parts. Market indexes stake claim to this key characteristic; custom indexes cannot make the same claim, as they are strategies with no regard to their constituent parts. An example of how constituent indexes sum to form a broad-market index is the Russell 3000 Index, which represents nearly 98 percent of the investable U.S. equity market. By drilling down, you can divide the Russell 3000 Index into the Russell 1000 Index, which represents 1,000 large-cap stocks, and the Russell 2000 Index, which represents 2,000 small-cap stocks.

Major Index Sponsors

Although there are dozens of index sponsors, seven major market index sponsors dominate the marketplace. These include Standard and Poor's, Dow Jones Indexes (DJI), MSCI (formerly Morgan Stanley Capital International), Russell Investments, Barclays Global Investors, Wilshire Associates, and Morningstar Associates (see Figure 1-9).

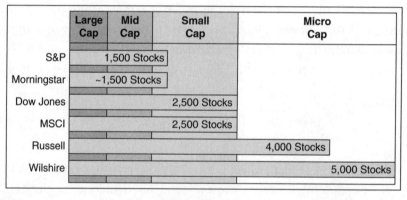

	Large Cap	Mid Cap	Small Cap	Micro Cap
S&P	1,500 Stocks			
Morningstar	~1,500 Stocks			
Dow Jones			2,500 Stocks	
MSCI			2,500 Stocks	
Russell				4,000 Stocks
Wilshire				5,000 Stocks

Figure 1-9 **Simplified U.S. Market Capitalization Representation by Index Sponsor**

CHAPTER 2

ETF Essentials and Distinctive Mechanics

We now turn our attention to the more detailed aspects of ETFs, namely the defining attributes, leading misconceptions, and distinctive features, with special emphasis on the creation and redemption process. This chapter can best be described as "looking to see what's under the hood" of an ETF. Some of the concepts and ideas may appear to be technical, but I think there's a good balance between descriptions of the material in technical language and toned-down "normal speak." We start off with the defining attributes of ETFs.

DEFINING ATTRIBUTES OF ETFs

Very specific and definable attributes underlie any investing concept or strategy. ETFs are no different. As Figure 2-1 shows, ETFs can be defined easily by a number of different attributes that present them in a unique light. Although we will discuss each one of these attributes in varying degrees in this book, this section will present the most important of the attributes to showcase their importance

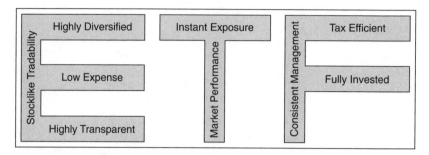

Figure 2-1 **Defining Attributes of ETFs**

and compelling benefits. This is a key section for someone who wants to understand why he or she should invest in ETFs, since it will outline the specific reasons for doing so. Note that there are other attributes to ETFs—such as having no minimum initial purchase requirements—but these are considered to be not as important as the following defining attributes, which are presented in no particular order.

ETFs Are Highly Diversified

ETFs may trade like stocks, but they resemble mutual funds in many more ways than they do stocks. The most important resemblance to mutual funds is their highly diversified nature. By combining dozens or even hundreds of stocks into one investment (e.g., the Vanguard Small-Cap ETF has over 1,700 underlying stocks), an ETF provides an incredibly diversified investment within its particular market segment. As a result, an ETF minimizes investment-specific risk associated with a single stock held in the fund. This advantage is important since it safeguards a portfolio from significant losses attributed to investment-specific events, such as mismanagement by a company's CEO (e.g., Enron), at-fault environmental disasters (e.g., BP), or default in a corporate bond from a single issuer (e.g., General Motors). (Figure 2-2 shows the benefits of portfolio diversification.)

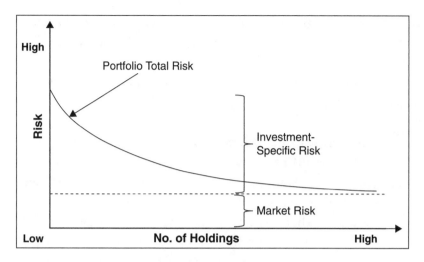

Figure 2-2 **Benefits of Portfolio Diversification**

Research clearly demonstrates that diversification benefits begin to occur when a portfolio holds 15 to 20 stocks. However, for best results, the stocks need to be of similar nature and within a similar market segment. Holding stocks in different industries does not provide the same level of benefit as does holding multiple stocks in the same industry. ETFs by nature follow this approach. Holding stocks in the same industry should not be a concern at this level if proper asset allocation is followed. Asset allocation and diversification are not the same thing; both strategies should be pursued for maximum results.

ETFs Offer Instant Exposure

As with mutual funds, ETFs provide investors with a means to gain instant exposure to a desired asset class or market segment. By simply purchasing one ETF, an investor is able to gain proportional ownership in each one of the underlying holdings, which can be in the hundreds to thousands of stocks. If you were to build a portfolio of individual stocks, it would take multiple stocks—and the time it takes to purchase them—to gain material exposure to a particular market segment. For example, purchasing IBM and Google does not assure you of appropriate exposure to the technology sector. However, an ETF that comprises both IBM and Google, as well as dozens of additional technology stocks, will provide the exposure you desire.

Many portfolio managers who build portfolios with individual stocks use ETFs to gain exposure to specific market segments quickly and easily. For example, if a certain portfolio manager believes the Wednesday crude oil inventory report will show much lower inventories than expected, then she can purchase the XLE (Energy Select Sector SPDR) in the hope of generating incremental gains without needing to research and purchase various individual energy-linked stocks.

ETFs Offer Stocklike Tradability

One of the first advantages that casual investors recognize is the stocklike tradability offered by ETFs. Although mutual funds are rather constrained by how a shareholder can transact, the same is not true with ETFs. The original blueprint for ETFs called for a significant emphasis on stocklike tradability in order to go head-to-head with stocks and attract new assets under management and new revenues for both ETF providers and stock exchanges. Stocklike tradability affords shareholders the ability to execute any number of discretionary order types long reserved for stock investors. These order types include market orders, limit orders, stop-loss orders, buying on margin, and selling short. Individual brokerage firms expand on this list with their own proprietary order types.

ETFs Are Highly Transparent

Transparency of fund holdings and applicable costs is essential to evaluating and investing in the most appropriate ETF. In addition to mutual funds not providing a satisfactory level of transparency, their fund-level disclosures are not at all on the same level as that of ETFs. Shareholders have the ability to investigate the holdings of an ETF on a daily basis. Furthermore, they also have the confidence and knowledge of the expenses of the ETF on both the fund level and portfolio level. Shareholders demand to get what they pay for, and full transparency ensures they achieve that aim.

ETFs Are Tax Efficient

Mutual funds are notorious for passing through fund-level capital gains tax liabilities that derive from partial or complete liquidations of underlying securities with embedded unrealized gains. Even if you did not sell your mutual fund, you as a shareholder in the fund can be responsible for a capital gains tax liability—typically distributed late in the year to shareholders of record as of a certain date prior to the distribution date. Mutual funds are required to make distributions of capital gains and losses, since mutual funds are considered pass-through pooled investments. If a mutual fund were not to distribute capital gains, then the mutual fund itself would be responsible for footing the tax bill.

Building up capital gains and then distributing them to shareholders rarely happens with ETFs, given their tax-friendly structure. Tax deferral with an ETF is a natural result of Subchapter M of the Internal Revenue Code, which permits fund redemptions in kind without triggering a taxable event inside the fund.

In addition to the negative consequence of recognizing capital gains, built-up unrealized capital gains on the fund level can also pose a serious problem, specifically its influence on the behavior of mutual fund portfolio managers. This problem can create a situation that adversely impacts tax-exempt investors and puts them at a disadvantage compared with taxable investors. For instance, if a mutual fund has a sizable built-up unrealized gain, then the portfolio manager may decide not to sell a security to avoid recognizing capital gains even though the security is considered fairly valued and deserving of being liquidated and the proceeds reinvested elsewhere.

ETFs Are Fully Invested

Many shareholders may not be aware of the fact that most mutual funds are not fully invested and therefore hold a modest to significant cash position. This is necessary not only to satisfy mutual fund shareholder liquidations but also for tactical asset allocation purposes. Higher-than-expected investment inflows can also lead to abnormally high cash balances. Irrespective of the reason why this is so, holding cash on the fund level translates to an unintended asset mix that overweights fixed income at the expense of equities, thus giving control over asset allocation policy to an outside party. Since ETFs do not have to satisfy shareholder liquidations, ETF providers can choose to be fully invested without the need to consider the ramifications a mutual fund would face in the same situation. An ETF that is fully invested takes advantage of rising markets rather than having cash sit idle and not participate in stock market rallies.

ETFs Deliver Market Performance

One of the most striking disadvantages of mutual funds and other actively managed investments is their historical underperformance against appropriate benchmarks. Research has clearly demonstrated that most actively managed investments do not outperform their relative benchmarks in any given year, and when they do outperform, the likelihood of them repeating this achievement is lower. All active managers outperforming their relative benchmark want you and other shareholders to believe they possess truly special investing skills and judgment. From a mathematical perspective, someone is always going to outperform—some with consistency year after year. In contrast, ETFs do not worry about generating alpha, or outperformance, since many ETFs focus on generating beta, or market returns. Any difference between the underlying index and the ETF is a result of tracking error. As previously mentioned, the ideal ETFs have the smallest margin of tracking error. This may seem somewhat boring, but when you consider the higher costs and less favorable tax efficiency that

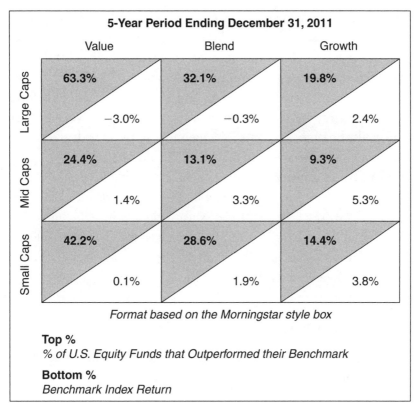

Figure 2-3 **Active Versus Passive Performance**

you get with mutual funds, acceptance of market performance isn't so bad after all. See Figure 2-3 for a comparison of active management performance versus passive management performance.

ETFs Offer Consistent Management

Have you ever heard the term *style drift* before? It refers to the tendency of a portfolio manager to deviate from his or her fund's specific strategy or objective. For example, a portfolio manager running a large-cap mutual fund might include some mid-cap stocks. I trust this is done with the best intentions—to make shareholders money. But decisions to alter an objective should be done on the individual portfolio level by investors and not on the fund level by portfolio managers, especially those you have never spoken to or met before. Investors are best able to design and rebalance their portfolios to meet their needs and objectives rather than defer this work to someone they have never seen, talked to, or perhaps even heard of before.

Style drift is more common than you might think. No, it doesn't happen all the time, nor does it happen to a significant degree when it does happen. Passively managed ETFs do not fall prey to this pitfall and offer a steadfast management style. That is because ETFs do not have portfolio managers who can make ad hoc decisions; instead, ETFs track known indexes using sophisticated computers. When building a portfolio of multiple asset classes, having confidence that your investments are what they say they are provides assurance in your portfolio and its ability to achieve the results you desire.

ETFs Are Low Expense

One of the most important defining attributes underlying ETFs is their favorable cost structure, especially in comparison with mutual funds. ETFs typically have significantly lower expense ratios than comparable mutual funds (see Figure 2-4) as well as no up-front or back-end sales loads. Furthermore, ETFs shareholders are not faced with subsidy trading costs, also known as *cost of flow*, which are the fund-level trading costs the remaining shareholders must pay when another shareholder exits a fund. The absence of subsidy costs (around 0.75 percent annually as determined by a 2007 study by Roger Edelen, Richard Evans, and Gregory Kadlec) provides protection to shareholders over and above anything available with mutual funds. Because ETF shareholders do not have to pay subsidy trading costs for other shareholders, the performance realized by an ETF shareholder should, over time, be significantly higher than the performance realized by a shareholder in an otherwise comparable mutual fund, whether actively or passively managed. Additionally, one of the indirect benefits of not having subsidy trading costs is a fully invested ETF. Low expenses are critical, since small annual differences add up to substantial savings over many years.

| Range | | % of ETFs |
From	To	
0.000%	0.404%	31.7%
0.404%	0.748%	39.0%
0.748%	1.092%	28.0%
1.092%	3.500%	1.3%
Average Mutual Fund Expense Ratio		1.50%

Figure 2-4 **Expense Ratio Snapshot**

CREATIONS AND REDEMPTIONS

The key to what makes ETFs so different from any other investment —especially mutual funds—is the creation and redemption process. This process is so vitally important that without it ETFs would not resemble anything like they do today and instead would closely resemble closed-end funds. The creation and redemption process affords ETFs the ability to be less expensive, more transparent, tradable without premiums and discounts, fully invested, and more tax efficient than nearly all other investments in the marketplace today. But what exactly is the creation and redemption process, and why is it so unique and important?

Background

Before the advent of ETFs, investment funds traded with a premium or discount to their net asset value (NAV). To avoid this inherent and undesirable flaw under then-existing models, ETF providers envisioned a process wherein no premiums and discounts would exist since they would be arbitraged away quickly and easily by independent third-party money managers. Why third party? The reason is that ETF providers realized that any involvement in the trading of underlying securities could create conflicts of interest—whether fictional or factual —and thus derail any innovation that relied on the creation and redemption process. Consequently, the plan was to rely on outside third-party money managers—such as Merrill Lynch, Goldman Sachs, and Morgan Stanley—to decide when new ETF shares would be issued and when existing ETF shares would be redeemed in accordance with an ETF framework. In due time, these outside third-party money managers became known as authorized participants (APs).

Although their role is exceedingly important, from an inside perspective their role is nearly free of risk—something we refer to as "arbitrage." In their designed role, APs buy and sell shares to ensure there are no premiums or discounts. The original designers of ETFs were not stupid; they realized that involving the work of multiple competing APs was essential to the competitiveness and credibility of the process. Therefore, there are times when both Morgan Stanley and Goldman Sachs will each execute arbitrage transactions in the same ETF, thus reducing the potential for conflicts of interest, providing for greater transparency, and ultimately leading to reasonable arbitrage profits. *Reasonable* is the catchword here since it makes no sense to create an investment where the bulk of the profits go to a firm rather than to the shareholders. Government watchdogs observe all aspects of the creation and redemption process.

The Process

When ETFs are created, APs are involved with either buying or borrowing the appropriate basket of securities underlying an ETF and exchanging them with the ETF provider for what are called "creation units" (see Figure 2-5). The creation units comprise large blocks of tens of thousands of ETF shares and must be equal to the NAV published holdings from the previous market close. In doing so, the ETF provider is prevented from indirectly profiting from the share creation and redemption process since the closing NAV is a known quantity. This safeguard satisfies the SEC's concern for potential abuse within the process.

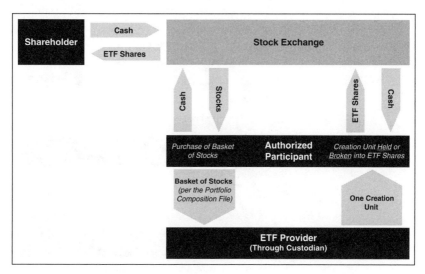

Figure 2-5 **Simplified Creation Process**

When an AP delivers a basket of underlying securities and related cash to the ETF provider (through the custodian bank), the AP in turn receives one creation unit issued by the provider through the designated custodian. These creation units are typically large blocks of ETF shares—usually up to 50,000—but they can be as high as 600,000 and as low as 20,000. Upon receiving creation units, an AP has the option of holding the units or selling some or all outright in the open market, perhaps to another AP. The AP may even go the route of breaking up creation units into individual ETF shares underlying the fund where they are sold to shareholders throughout the day on a stock exchange. ETF providers may permit an AP to substitute cash for some or all of the securities underlying a creation unit when the securities are difficult to obtain or not held by certain types of investors.

When a shareholder sells shares of his or her ETF, or when there is a divergence between the market price and the NAV, then the process goes into reverse order (see Figure 2-6). With redemptions, an AP purchases shares of an ETF on the open market, forms a creation unit (or "redemption basket") in accordance with the requirements, and delivers the creation unit to the ETF provider.

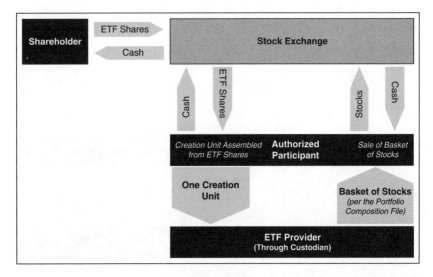

Figure 2-6 **Simplified Redemption Process**

Upon delivery of the creation unit, the AP receives individual securities and related cash equal to the exact NAV comprising the creation unit. ETF providers typically assess a fee to an AP based on the quantity of creation units created or redeemed. The amount is rather low—typically $1,000 per 50,000-share transaction—but high enough when multiplied by the number of units transacted to give ETF providers incremental revenues to pay for work involved with the creation and redemption process.

So how do APs know which securities underlying an ETF to include in the basket they turn over to ETF providers in exchange for creation units? Actually, the process is much more refined and fluid than one might envision. Upon the close of each trading session, an ETF provider publishes what is called a "portfolio composition file," or PCF for short. These data tell an AP what securities—including the quantity—and what amount of cash are required to receive one creation unit. The timing and accuracy of the data are essential to ensure that the creation and redemption process runs smoothly.

A third-party organization called the National Securities Clearing Corporation (NSCC) is charged with the responsibility of accepting, processing, and disseminating all PCFs to interested

APs prior to the opening of the market on the following trading session. Any changes in the composition of the market index being tracked can be accommodated between an ETF provider and AP through PCFs. For instance, when the underlying securities in an ETF are revised, and thus the creation unit is altered, an AP will deliver the newly added security to the ETF provider and receive in return the security that was removed—all via the custodian bank.

Technically speaking, it is not the ETF provider that is selling the shares; instead, it is the authorized participant that takes on this function. As a result, shareholders have no direct relationship with the ETF provider itself. This difference is trivial in nature, but one worth mentioning nonetheless.

Role of Authorized Participants

An authorized participant is involved both when the new ETFs start up and when the demand for transacting shares of an existing ETF increases. An AP's job is to facilitate the creation and redemption of shares underlying an ETF. The "in-kind" exchange of a basket of stock comprising the underlying securities and creation units takes place on a one-for-one, fair-value basis. Specifically, the AP delivers a certain amount of underlying securities, or basket of stocks, and receives the exact same value in ETF shares—based on the NAV and not the market value of the ETF at that particular moment. As a result, both parties benefit from the transaction. The ETF provider receives the securities it needs to track the index, and the authorized participant receives a corresponding number of ETF creation units to hold or resell for profit.

Likewise, when a shareholder is selling his or her investment, an AP removes ETF shares from the open market by purchasing an equivalent amount of shares to form a creation unit and then delivers the creation unit to the ETF provider. In exchange, the AP receives the same value in the underlying securities of the ETF.

So how do APs profit from the creation and redemption process and what gives them the financial incentive to be involved? The primary way is to gain from the arbitrage transactions needed to eliminate the premiums and discounts on the fund level and make risk-free profits in the process. For instance, when an ETF is selling at a premium to its underlying NAV, then an AP—perhaps multiple APs—will step in and sell shares of the ETF on the open market and simultaneously buy shares of the underlying securities. Thereafter the AP will exchange with the ETF provider the recently purchased underlying shares of securities for creation units. The AP continues this process until the market price for the ETF is in line with the NAV of the ETF. Although this process may appear cumbersome and time consuming, it really is not. Sophisticated computers facilitate the purchases and sales by using detailed and explicit models, making for a quick and easy process. The ultimate result is a properly aligned ETF with risk-free profits to the AP.

Importance of the Creation and Redemption Process

The creation and redemption process is vitally important in regard to ETFs for three key reasons. These reasons are provided below with detailed explanations following the bulleted summaries:

- It eliminates trading premiums and discounts by keeping all ETF market prices and their corresponding NAVs in line with each other.
- It prevents existing shareholders from having to pay transaction costs (both subsidy and AP) for transactions of others.
- It avoids financial conflicts of interest (specifically abusive trading practices and unacceptable arbitrage profits) because of the involvement of APs.

First, the creation and redemption process ensures that the ETF share price trades in line with the underlying NAV. Without this advantage, an ETF would trade much like a glorified closed-end fund with either a premium or discount. Since an ETF has stocklike tradability, the price for an ETF fluctuates during trading sessions—due to supply and demand fundamentals. As such, when an ETF becomes more expensive than the sum of its underlying securities, an AP can sell shares of the ETF and purchase and deliver underlying securities to the ETF provider—thus receiving a creation unit—and exchange that creation unit outright or sell the ETF shares on the open market. This process returns the market price for an ETF back to its NAV. Likewise, if the underlying securities become more expensive than the ETF market price, then the AP can purchase shares of the ETF equivalent to the value of a creation unit and redeem them for the underlying securities, which can be sold in the open market. The ultimate result of the arbitrage creation and redemption process is an ETF market price that trades in line with its underlying NAV.

Second, the creation and redemption process ensures that current shareholders do not pay for transactions executed by either market-timing investors or APs in conjunction with their arbitrage role. As a result, ETFs are extraordinarily efficient and fair for all involved participants. In contrast, when mutual fund shareholders invest new money, the fund company must take that money and purchase underlying securities in the open market. This unfortunately translates into higher costs for all shareholders. And as we all know, higher costs ultimately harm returns. The same process occurs when shareholders withdraw their money from a mutual fund. Fortunately, ETFs are much different, as APs do much of the buying and selling and incur the bulk of the trading costs, whether explicit or implicit. APs typically pay all the trading costs and fees, including additional fees to the ETF provider for the "paperwork" involved in processing all of the creations and redemptions. As a result, the ETF system shifts the burden of underlying trading costs associated with shareholder transactions to the AP and away from the ETF. This is not true for mutual funds, in which the fund and therefore existing shareholders pay costs—subsidy trading costs—when other shareholders sell their positions. The mutual fund in this case bears the trading cost without regard for a specific shareholder. Nonetheless, ETFs can be responsible for picking up the tab for nonshareholder transactions such as an index change where a constituent security is being replaced by another and the ETF is required to make related revisions.

Third, the creation and redemption process ensures that financial conflicts of interest are eliminated since all underlying securities and their weightings are known by way of the portfolio composition file. In addition, because multiple APs are contracted, there is greater competition among APs to ensure that the process operates as needed. As we all know from Economics 101, greater competition typically equates to smaller margins—or, in this case, mutually acceptable arbitrage profits. If an ETF provider engaged only one AP, the opportunity to capture unacceptably high arbitrage profits—at the expense of shareholders—and having greater discretion over when and to what degree to buy or sell the underlying securities would be otherwise more common.

ETF VALUATION CONSIDERATIONS

This section is dedicated to topics that relate to ETF valuation and the metrics that help to define value. The four most important valuation considerations are market price, net asset value, tracking error, and liquidity (which is oftentimes misunderstood by investors). We start off by investigating the intricacies of market price.

Market Price

Market price refers to the last price at which an ETF was transacted, which can be the bid price, ask price (also known as the offer price), or somewhere in between. Bid and ask prices provide the pricing level at which 100 shares or more of an ETF are available for transaction: at least 100 shares at the bid or selling price and 100 at the ask or purchase price. The difference between the two is called the "bid-ask spread" or "trading spread." The market price reflects the best-known price for an ETF and is therefore used in many valuation calculations such as market capitalization.

Some ETFs trade with relatively narrow spreads, whereas others trade with wide ones. Although investor demand and supply does play a minor role in determining the trading spread, the leading determinant of ETF trading spreads arises from the spreads of the underlying securities. As a result, ETFs that hold highly liquid securities with narrow spreads on average will tend to exhibit narrow spreads themselves, all else being equal. ETFs that track blue-chip companies, such as the Dow Jones Industrial Average (DJIA), will enjoy this advantage. Other ETFs, especially those that track emerging markets, will find their own spreads to be wider than others given the wider spreads of the underlying stocks.

One of the significant benefits of ETFs is the involvement of APs to arbitrage and bring the spread in line with the spreads of the underlying stocks. Without this risk-free trading, ETF spreads would deviate from the underlying spreads, and that could mean wider spreads on the fund level and thus higher trading costs.

Finally, ETF spreads are not static; they are constantly moving in response to how the market is behaving and how trading is impacting the spreads of the underlying securities. When there is added risk in the market as a result of geopolitical events, spreads typically widen. Conversely, a calm and benign few days in the market can cause spreads to narrow.

Net Asset Value

Net asset value is a term used to describe the accounting value for an ETF on a per-share basis. The calculation for NAV is quite simple: The fund's assets less liabilities are divided by the number of shares outstanding. The result is expressed in dollar terms. Mutual funds use NAV as well and calculate the value in the same manner as ETFs.

Calculating NAV is the work of a fund accounting group, sometimes called "portfolio accounting group." The computer systems used by fund accounting groups are rather sophisticated and are used to account for investment inflows and outflows, purchases and sales of the underlying securities, fund operating expenses, and any security-specific income, gains, and losses. Once the valuation process is complete and all accounting entries are posted, then the accounting books are considered "closed," thus enabling the NAV per share to be calculated and disseminated to the marketplace. Although both ETFs and mutual funds employ this same system, ETFs also provide an intraday real-time estimate of current valuation appropriately called "intraday indicative value" (IIV). This value per share is published every 15 seconds for both investors and APs alike to view. This value is essential, given that ETFs trade continuously throughout the day and are not transacted at the close of trading at a fund's NAV price as are mutual funds.

Tracking Error

Tracking error is a ratio expressed as a percentage that measures the unplanned deviation of return generated by an ETF compared to the return of an index benchmark over a fixed period of time. Over time, the greater the use of passive management, the smaller the tracking error tends to be. Tracking error is expressed as either a positive number (for outperformance of the ETF) or a negative number (which represents underperformance). Deviations between the returns are generally very small and thus expressed in basis points rather than full percentage points.

Many years ago, analysis of ETFs with tracking error was not done to a significant degree because of the low number of indexes tracked. However, as ETFs began to track greater numbers of indexes, the need to analyze, evaluate, and compare ETFs became much more important. Although there are several different methods for calculating tracking error, the most widely accepted one is the difference between the NAV return of the ETF and the return of the index being tracked. Because ETF market values converge to the NAV over time, any differences between NAV return and ETF return are insignificant.

One of the final pieces to the puzzle for calculating tracking error is whether or not to include expense ratio costs. From the perspective of some within the ETF marketplace, expense ratios are outside the benchmarking of an ETF and thus not a true factor in explaining any difference in net returns. In consequence, expense ratios should be added back to arrive at a more investment-centric measure. However, from the perspective of ETF shareholders, the expense ratio cost is an actual cost that must be paid in order to invest in ETFs; it helps to better compare ETFs. Therefore, ETF investors are better served by keeping the cost in the calculation. Low-cost ETF providers prefer the cost to be included as well, since it helps their cause by showing lower tracking error than their peers' tracking error, all else being equal.

Some ETFs produce small tracking error, and others produce larger tracking error. When tracking error is abnormally large for the index tracked, it is generally attributed to one or more of the following three reasons:

1. Difficulty in tracking an index due to illiquid index constituents
2. Difficulty in tracking an index due to sampling and optimization snags—particularly with small-cap stocks—given indexes with unusually large numbers of index constituents
3. Cash drag arising from ETF providers who, for various reasons, decide not to fully invest the cash within an ETF

Liquidity

ETFs were originally viewed as being more liquid than traditional mutual funds due to their stocklike tradability. Although this is true in aggregate, it is not necessarily true in all cases. Why is greater liquidity more favorable? The reason is that lower levels of liquidity can lead to wider ETF bid-ask spreads (i.e. higher trading costs), wider divergences between an ETF's market value and the value of its underlying stocks, and reduced ability to trade quickly and easily.

The level of liquidity for an ETF is based on four factors. First and most important, ETF liquidity is determined by the liquidity of the underlying securities. Large blue-chip names will provide excellent liquidity, whereas emerging market stocks and REITs provide much less. The place where securities are listed—the exchange and the country—also impacts underlying securities and their related liquidity.

Second, ETF liquidity is influenced by the trading volume of the underlying securities. Securities with higher trading volumes will enable quick and easy transactions, ultimately translating into greater liquidity. Stocks with lower trading volumes have wider spreads and provide less favorable opportunities to buy and sell. This all trickles up to the fund level.

Third, ETF liquidity is influenced to a small degree by the trading volume of the ETF itself. The more buying and selling going on with an ETF, the more liquid the ETF tends to be.

Fourth, ETF liquidity is influenced by the perceived investment opportunity for the underlying securities. For example, when crude oil is rising, then there are more investors interested in purchasing energy stocks. Likewise, when an economy is believed to be coming out of a recession, there is a shift from consumer staple stocks to consumer discretionary stocks.

THE KNOWN (AND NOT-SO KNOWN) COSTS OF ETFs

One of the most important differences between ETFs and mutual funds is the total cost a shareholder pays to own the fund. Most shareholders are keenly aware that an ETF is lower cost, if not significantly lower cost, than a comparable mutual fund. However, even though ETFs are cost favorable, that does not mean they are free—there are costs that must be paid. Some of these costs are highly transparent, while others are much less so. Furthermore, costs can be grouped according to where they are assessed (e.g., at the fund level or shareholder level) and whether or not the costs impact tracking error (see Figure 2-7). If costs do impact tracking error, then they are appropriately called "tracking costs."

Tracking Costs	
Cost	**Assessment**
Expense Ratios	Fund Level
Dividend Drag	Fund Level
Cash Drag	Fund Level
Trading Transparency	Fund Level
Tracking Snags	Fund Level
Non-Tracking Costs	
Cost	**Assessment**
Commissions	Shareholder Level
Bid-Ask Spreads	Shareholder Level
Premiums	Shareholder Level
Taxation	Shareholder Level

Figure 2-7 **Overview of ETF Costs**

Tracking Costs

This section highlights internal costs incurred on the fund level that impact how closely an ETF tracks its underlying index. For most ETFs, higher costs mean greater tracking error, and lower costs mean less tracking error—which of course is the main objective. The primary tracking costs include expense ratios, dividend drag, cash drag, trading transparency, and tracking snags.

Expense Ratios

The most transparent tracking cost you will pay when investing in an ETF is the expense ratio, called "MER" (management expense ratio) in Europe. An expense ratio is expressed in percentage terms, assessed on the market value of the ETF, and paid by shareholders on a pro rata basis daily. Operating costs are the most significant component of expense ratios, but also included are other costs incurred by an ETF provider, such as royalty fees (i.e., ongoing fees paid to index sponsors to track and market their indexes).

When you compare funds of similar investment style and objectives, ETFs have much lower expense ratios than comparable mutual funds. One of the reasons explaining this fact is the existence of expenses known as 12b-1 fees (typically 0.25 percent of market value)—assessed by many mutual funds to compensate investment professionals for serving (i.e., keeping) shareholders in their funds. Mutual fund companies refer to this fee as a service or marketing fee. ETFs do not charge 12b-1 fees.

Dividend Drag

Dividend drag refers to the implicit cost some ETFs (e.g., unit investment trusts) incur as a result of SEC rules stipulating that these ETFs cannot immediately reinvest dividends paid by companies held by the ETF back into the fund. Instead, some ETFs must accumulate the dividends in a cash reserve account and pay them to shareholders at periodic intervals, typically quarterly. This requirement differs for most mutual funds and ETFs legally structured as open-end funds, as they can reinvest dividends immediately. When the equity market is doing well, dividends are better served being reinvested rather than held back until paid out on specific dates. This drawback with some ETFs creates a performance penalty and ultimately a drag on returns that otherwise would not have occurred had the dividend been reinvested at the time of payment by an underlying stock.

Cash Drag

Cash drag refers to the loss of potential performance as a result of an ETF not being fully invested. The vast majority of ETFs are fully invested since they do not have to satisfy shareholder withdrawal requests—a normal fact of life for mutual funds. Nonetheless, there are times, although infrequent, when ETFs are not fully invested even though there has been nothing holding the fund back from investing all available cash. As with dividend drag, when markets are rising, cash is better served being invested and not idle, making only a fraction of what could be earned in the stock market.

Trading Transparency

Trading transparency refers to the implicit costs that passively managed ETFs incur as a result of needing to rebalance given preannounced index reconstitutions. Once an index sponsor preannounces upcoming changes to a market index, then speculators (known in practice as scalpers) can front-run any ETF provider by purchasing the security being added to an index and selling short the security being removed—all before the index is officially reconstituted and ETFs can make their change. These front-running transactions drive up costs for an ETF that needs to make changes to mirror the underlying market index. The cost is embedded in the fund and not easily identified or quantified by shareholders.

Tracking Snags

Tracking snags can be very problematic—and costly—for ETFs that track market indexes. This cost, along with the expense ratio cost, is the leading factor explaining tracking error. One of the most common issues arising with ETFs in regard to tracking snags is the difficulty of replicating a market index that contains either illiquid securities or a significant number of securities, particularly small-cap stocks. Illiquid securities can cause transaction timing delays and may mean higher costs to transact. Additionally, when a market index contains an exceptionally large number of securities, an ETF provider can—with the exception of unit investment trust structures—and will typically employ a sampling method to replicate the index to reduce custodial and administrative costs. However, since sampling and optimization methods typically underweight small-cap stocks, then the ETF will outperform the index when small caps underperform; they will underperform when small caps outperform. Irrespective of the catalyst, tracking error attributed to index replication snags is a real cost to ETF shareholders and is incurred on the fund level.

Nontracking Costs

Costs incurred on the shareholder level that do not impact how closely an ETF tracks its underlying index are appropriately called "nontracking costs." The primary nontracking costs include commissions, bid-ask (or trading) spreads, premiums (to NAV), and taxes.

Commissions

Unlike mutual funds, ETFs are exclusively purchased and sold via traditional brokerage firms, not through the providers themselves, with the exception of a couple of providers. These brokerage firms want to get paid for their efforts and therefore charge trading commissions, including transactions for buying and selling ETFs. Buy and sell transactions are typically not assessed commissions with mutual funds, but this is because some funds charge up-front or back-end loads, or commissions, while all mutual funds bake shareholder trading costs into their fund, which ultimately impacts a fund's NAV. Nonetheless, having a transparent expense is always preferable to a hidden and unknown fee.

Additionally, many brokerage firms—namely, Fidelity Investments, TD Ameritrade, Charles Schwab, Scottrade, and Vanguard—now offer commission-free trading on select ETFs to attract more investors and additional assets under management. When a shareholder desires to purchase an ETF, he or she executes a transaction with a brokerage firm. ETFs listed on the New York Stock Exchange typically have three-letter symbols, while the Nasdaq generally issues ETF symbols with four letters.

Bid-Ask Spreads

Bid-ask spreads, also referred to as trading spreads, are best defined as the difference between the price at which an investor sells a security and the price at which the counterparty investor purchases the security. Given their tradability on stock exchanges, all ETFs by nature trade with bid-ask spreads. There is simply no way around this cost. As a result, one-half of the bid-ask spread is a cost when you purchase an ETF, and the other half is the cost when you sell an ETF.

For the most part, bid-ask spreads are quite small and completely transparent. There is no hiding either bid and ask prices or the corresponding spread in between. As mentioned previously in this chapter, the spread between the bid price and ask price is dictated by an ETF's liquidity, which itself is based on the spreads of the underlying stocks. More liquid ETFs trade with narrower spreads (just pennies per share), whereas less liquid ETFs have wider spreads—sometimes reaching over $0.50 per share.

Knowing the spread is very important since it arms you with the ability to cut the spread with a limit order to buy or sell rather than entering a market order and accepting the spread as is. Mutual funds do not have bid-ask spreads on the fund level and therefore present a distinct advantage over ETFs in this regard. This is because mutual funds are not purchased or sold on a stock exchange and instead are transacted at the end-of-day price, which is the net asset value. No matter how you slice it, the spread you pay to purchase or sell an ETF is a cost that simply cannot be avoided.

Premiums

Premiums and discounts are nonexistent with mutual funds since shareholders transact at the net asset value. Premiums and discounts are most widely associated with closed-end funds. Consequently, most closed-end funds trade either at discounts to NAV or at premiums to NAV. As for ETFs, premiums and discounts are typically a nonissue, given the creation and redemption process via arbitrage trades by APs. Nonetheless, premiums and discounts do exist for some ETFs and sometimes for extended periods of time. Non–Treasury bond ETFs are the most susceptible due to either illiquidity of underlying fixed-income securities and/or to uncontrollable external factors such as the halt of the creations and redemption process attributed to regulatory scrutiny. International ETFs are more susceptible to the occurrence of premiums than are U.S. ETFs.

Taxes

The favorable tax treatment afforded ETFs is one of the top two reasons for investing in ETFs over comparable mutual funds. Unlike mutual funds, ETFs have inherent efficiencies due to the creation and redemption process, where little to no capital gains tax liability is incurred. Of course, the tax liability depends on the type of ETF, since currency, leveraged/or inverse, and (most importantly) commodities-linked holdings have less-favorable tax treatment. Most plain-vanilla ETFs have never made a capital gains distribution in their existence—a claim very few mutual funds can make. For tax-exempt investors, capital gains are a nonissue since they are reinvested with no outflow of capital to pay taxes. However, fully taxable investors cannot say the same thing. Furthermore, mutual fund portfolio managers can find themselves in tricky situations when they must decide between selling an overvalued underlying security with unrealized gains and holding the security to avoid triggering capital gains taxes.

Leveraged and inverse ETFs have paid out substantial capital gains, and so too have currency-linked ETFs. Not knowing this difference between ETFs can get investors in trouble and expose them to unintended taxes. For instance, most investors do not know that investing in precious metals ETFs, such as the massive SPDR Gold Shares (symbol: GLD), will mean that capital gains are taxed at a 28 percent rate because precious metals are considered collectibles. Additionally, most investors are not aware of the tax provisions of commodity investing. According to Internal Revenue Service (IRS) rules, gains arising from an ETF in which the underlying securities are commodity futures are taxed as 60 percent long-term gains and 40 percent short-term gains. Complicating the issue is the IRS rule stating that gains are considered marked to market (i.e., the gains were recognized at the end of the year and thus payable even though the investment had not been liquidated).

In addition to taxes on capital gains, taxes on dividends and interest are also quite common. This situation is nothing different from when one invests in mutual funds. When an underlying security pays a dividend or interest payment, the ETF will reinvest or accrue the income and pass through to shareholders on certain dates. Depending on the type of account involved, income is fully taxable and typically charged against the taxpayer's federal tax rate.

CHAPTER 3

The Expanding Universe of ETFs

The universe of ETFs encompasses six primary categories: broad-based style and size ETFs, sector and industry ETFs, global ETFs, fixed-income ETFs, real asset ETFs, and leveraged and inverse ETFs. Each category can be divided even further into subcategories and segments, thus providing investors with a full array of ETFs to choose from and to build a comprehensive ETF portfolio that stays true to an optimally allocated portfolio.

STYLE AND SIZE ETFs

Approximately half of Americans own common stock either directly or indirectly through mutual funds, exchange-traded funds, managed accounts, or insurance products. The number of Americans owning equities has ballooned over the last couple of decades, and the trend continues to rise year after year.

Equities are considered the core of any traditional investment portfolio. Broad-based equities can be divided into specific and fundamentally different categories based on size and style (i.e., growth or value). Each fundamental difference provides greater investment opportunities and additional ways to enhance a portfolio's inherent risk and return profile.

Equity assets represent an ownership interest in a corporation and signify a claim to a corporation's assets. In order to fund business operations, corporations first raise capital by issuing equity securities. Each share of stock owned gives an investor a proportional share of the corporation's profits, which are usually distributed in the form of dividends. In addition, owners of most equity securities are given voting rights. Voting rights allow you, for instance, to vote for a corporation's board of directors, approve or disapprove of employee stock option programs, or vote for or against acquisitions.

There are two forms of equity securities—preferred stock and common stock—with common stock being the more widely held security. Do not get caught up in the names of each equity stock, because owning preferred stock is not necessarily more desirable than owning "common" stock. Each type of stock offers its own benefits, and each is suitable for different types of investors. We will first explore preferred stock and then common stock.

Preferred Stock

Preferred stock, like common stock, represents ownership of a corporation but is still slightly different from common stock. Shareholders of preferred stock typically do not have voting rights. In exchange, shareholders receive a higher priority on the assets of the corporation in the event of liquidation due to bankruptcy. Furthermore, it is commonplace for shareholders of preferred stock to receive not only a higher-yielding dividend but also priority in receiving dividends over that of common stock shareholders. For example, if a corporation is having difficulty in meeting its dividend payments to both preferred and common stock shareholders, then the corporation must make dividend payments to the preferred stock shareholders first. Afterward, if enough cash remains, common stock shareholders will receive their dividend payments. Cumulative preferred is a type of preferred stock that has priority in receiving dividends over that of common stock. The cumulative provision obligates the corporation to pay all accumulated but unpaid dividends before dividends can be made to the shareholders of common stock.

Finally, many corporations issue what is called convertible preferred stock. This type of preferred stock is very similar to non-convertible preferred stock with one significant difference. Convertible preferred stock gives shareholders the option to convert their preferred shares into (i.e., exchange their stock for) a fixed number of common stock shares after a predetermined date. The market value of this type of preferred stock is more volatile since its value is influenced by the market value of the underlying common stock.

Common Stock

Common stock is the most widely used form of equity ownership across the globe. Common stock shareholders have voting rights and often participate in receiving profits in the form of dividends. However, not all corporations distribute profits in the form of dividends. Instead, some reinvest the dividends back into their companies in order to fund existing operations and planned expenditures.

Two of the most common broad-based classifications associated with common stock are style and size equities. Style refers to a certain stock as being growth or value oriented, while size refers to a certain stock as being large cap, mid cap, small cap, or even micro cap. The differences within each asset subclass exhibit their own unique risk and return trade-off profile. Growth stocks are stocks of companies that produce strong long-term earnings growth rates along with solid cash-flow, sales, and book-value growth rates. Value stocks, on the other hand, are stocks of companies with low stock prices in comparison with projected earnings, book value, and sales per share, among other less important defining variables. As a result of the differences between style and size stocks, correlations between the two are semifavorable and therefore provide a degree of diversification benefits. Figure 3-1 lists the metrics and their

Value Metric	Weighting	Growth Metric
Stock price to projected earnings	**50.0%**	Long-term projected-earnings growth rate
Stock price to book value per share	**12.5%**	Historical-earnings growth rate
Stock price to sales per share	**12.5%**	Sales growth rate
Stock price to cash flow per share	**12.5%**	Cash-flow growth rate
Dividend yield	**12.5%**	Book-value growth rate

Figure 3-1 **Morningstar Value Versus Growth Metrics**

respective weightings Morningstar employs to define and classify value and growth stocks.

Depending on the variable for each factor, Morningstar will assign a particular stock as growth, value, or core. A core stock is essentially a blended stock that does not exhibit material growth or value tendencies. These aforementioned rankings by Morningstar are the backbone of its stock and mutual fund star ranking system.

Since growth and value stocks do not move in perfect lock-step with each other, investors have the opportunity to improve the risk-adjusted return of their portfolio by allocating to both asset classes. Low-cost ETFs are excellent ways to accomplish this task.

In the past, companies were exclusively divided into large caps, mid caps, and small caps. However, as companies grew larger and stretched the limits of existing market capitalization cutoffs, the addition of mega caps and micro caps (and sometimes nano caps) became a necessity. Grouping companies into relevant categories is a rather subjective process since there is no official definition of, or full consensus about, the exact cutoff values. Some research companies set cutoffs based on percentiles, whereas others are based in nominal dollars.

Complicating the situation is the fact that market capitalizations are not static; they are constantly changing and growing larger over time. As a result, cutoffs for each category have been increased each decade or so to keep in line with present market values. For example, a company with a market capitalization of $1 billion or more was considered a large cap in 1950, but today that same market cap could be categorized as being either small cap or mid cap but nowhere close to being large cap. Different countries around the world also recognize different valuations for cutoffs. Again, there are no hard rules for defining companies based on size.

Nonetheless, the following are the most widely accepted current levels for stocks based on market capitalization value:

- Mega cap: Over $100 billion
- Large cap: $10 billion to $100 billion
- Mid cap: $1 billion to $10 billion
- Small cap: $100 million to $1 billion
- Micro cap: $10 million to $100 million
- Nano cap: Below $10 million

Volatility Risk and Correlations

There is little doubt that equity assets possess a high degree of risk. Moreover, some equity asset classes exhibit greater amounts of risk than do other equity asset classes. For example, small-cap stocks possess more risk than do large-cap stocks. However, additional risk means higher-return potential. The two go hand in hand. From a historical perspective, small caps and micro caps have experienced substantial volatility risk. Large caps and mid caps also exhibit volatility risk, but they exhibit less volatility because they are more mature companies within more efficient markets. By allocating to investments with low correlations, investors can reduce portfolio volatility and smooth out large market-value swings.

ETF Representation

Even though we have given relatively equal discussion to all size categories, there is no mistaking the substantially higher assets

No.	ETF	Symbol	Assets ($B)
1	SPDR S&P 500	SPY	$92.7
2	iShares S&P 500 Index	IVV	$25.8
3	PowerShares QQQ	QQQ	$24.8
4	Vanguard Total Stock Market ETF	VTI	$19.3
5	iShares Russell 1000 Growth Index	IWF	$14.0
6	iShares Russell 2000 Index	IWM	$13.0
7	SPDR Dow Jones Industrial Average	DIA	$11.1
8	iShares Russell 1000 Value Index	IWD	$10.9
9	iShares S&P MidCap 400 Index	IJH	$9.3
10	SPDR S&P MidCap 400	MDY	$8.9

Figure 3-2 **Top 10 Largest U.S. Broad-Based ETFs**

under management with large-cap ETFs than with mid-cap and small-cap ETFs. As of the beginning of 2011, large-cap ETFs boasted nearly $247 billion in AuM. A number such as this illustrates clear domination of the respective market segment (i.e., asset class size). Mid-cap ETFs and small and micro caps had approximately $58 billion and $54 billion AuM, respectively. Furthermore, growth-focused ETFs held about $46 billion and value-focused ETFs about $40 billion in AuM, differences that are not especially important between each other. See Figure 3-2 for a ranking of the top 10 largest broad-based ETFs.

SECTOR AND INDUSTRY ETFs

In addition, being able to be divided into broad-based size and style categories, equities can also be broken down into economic sectors and industry groups. The popularity of these more targeted groups has resulted in the strong growth of ETFs that track these equity segments. This is demonstrated by the fact that nearly 25 percent of all equity ETFs are sector and industry funds. Sector and industry funds track not only U.S. markets but also international ones. Because of that, investors have solid investing alternatives to protect and grow their portfolios. The first sector funds were introduced in 1998—called Select Sector SPDRs—by State Street Global Advisors based on the economic sectors as recognized by Standard & Poor's. Nowadays, Vanguard, PowerShares, WisdomTree, Rydex-SGI (now part of Guggenheim Partners), and a host of others also offer sector and industry ETFs.

There are three primary reasons for investing in sector and industry ETFs. First, these funds provide investors with the means necessary to fill any gaps they might have in their asset allocation. Second, these funds give investors the opportunities to invest in more defined areas when they believe excess returns can be generated over and above the overall equity market. For example, if an investor believed basic materials stocks were close to breaking out from a technical standpoint, then that investor could overweight basic materials by purchasing the Materials Select Sector SPDR (symbol: XLB). Although the S&P 500 does provide exposure to basic materials, an investor may feel compelled to increase his or her exposure to take full advantage of perceived underpriced segments in the equity market. Third, sector and industry ETFs allow casual and institutional investors the means to hedge a portfolio, specifically a concentrated-stock portfolio. For example, a recently retired executive from a high-tech firm may hold a significant block of shares in his or her former employer. If the cost basis on that stock is low, then the executive may want to employ advanced strategies such as selling short a technology-sector ETF to hedge the downside risk of the concentrated position, without selling the low-basis stock outright and, as a result, incurring a significant capital gains tax liability.

Sector ETFs have two primary drawbacks. First, most sector ETFs have higher expense ratios than a broadly diversified ETF. The difference is typically small and still lower than comparable mutual funds, but differences do exist nonetheless. Second, the use of sector funds could motivate an investor to design a less-than-optimal portfolio and may even induce more frequent trading than under normal situations. Investing in sector or industry funds should be accomplished within the context of an optimally allocated, low-cost, and tax-efficient strategy.

Sector and Industry Classification

There are thousands of stocks in the United States and many more in the international marketplace. With so many stocks available, it makes sense to classify them into orderly and definable groups for ease of comparison and analysis. Dow Jones Indexes and Standard & Poor's are by far the two most followed companies for their classification of stocks. Morningstar and a few other index sponsors provide their own proprietary methodologies as well.

Dow Jones Indexes

Dow Jones sector indexes include a diverse range of broad-market indexes available at the country, regional, and global levels. Each sector is defined by the Industry Classification Benchmark, a proprietary classification standard jointly maintained by Dow Jones Indexes and the FTSE Group. Under the Dow Jones methodology, a database of more than 60,000 global securities in 72 countries is classified according to one of four levels of specificity, including 10 broad industries, 19 supersectors, 41 sectors, and, at the most granular level, 114 subsectors.

The 10 broad industries together with their constituent sectors are listed here, which represent approximately 95 percent of U.S. market capitalization:

1. **Basic materials:** Chemicals, forest and paper, industrial metals and mining, and mining
2. **Consumer goods:** Automobiles and parts, beverages, food producers, household goods and home construction, leisure goods, personal goods, and tobacco
3. **Consumer services:** Food and drug retailers, general retailers, media, and travel and leisure
4. **Financials:** Banks, equity investment instruments, financial services, life insurance, nonequity investment instruments, nonlife insurance, real estate investment trusts, and real estate investment and services

5. **Healthcare:** Healthcare equipment and services and pharmaceuticals and biotechnology
6. **Industrials:** Aerospace and defense, construction and materials, electronic and electrical equipment, general industrials, industrial engineering, industrial transportation, and support services
7. **Oil and gas:** Alternative energy, oil and gas producers, and oil equipment and services
8. **Technology:** Software and computer services and technology hardware and equipment
9. **Telecommunications:** Fixed-line telecommunications and mobile telecommunications
10. **Utilities:** Electricity and gas, water, and multiutilities

Standard & Poor's

Introduced in cooperation with MSCI, the Global Industry Classification Standard (GICS) from Standard & Poor's contains data on well over 30,000 global stocks. Under this system, GICS divides the S&P 1500 Index into 10 economic sectors, 23 industry groups, 59 industries, and 123 subindustries. The following are the 10 economic sectors together with select constituent industries, according to Standard & Poor's:

1. **Basic materials:** Chemicals, metals and mining, and paper and forest products
2. **Consumer discretionary:** Automobiles, apparel, leisure, and media
3. **Consumer staples:** Food and drug retailing and household products
4. **Energy:** Energy equipment, oil and gas exploration, and refining
5. **Financials:** Banks, financial services, and all insurance
6. **Healthcare:** Biotech, drugs, managed care, and medical products

7. **Industrials:** Aerospace, building, capital goods, defense, and transportation
8. **Information technology:** Communication equipment, hardware, and software
9. **Telecommunication services:** Telecommunication services and wireless
10. **Utilities:** Electric utilities and natural gas utilities

Morningstar

Taking a rather different approach, Morningstar classifies companies according to the industry in which the company's business activities generate the bulk of its revenue. Depending on the source of revenue, companies are classified under one of Morningstar's 129 industries, which themselves are classified into 1 of 12 sectors. Morningstar does not stop there, as it further classifies the 12 sectors in 1 of 3 supersectors: information economy (about 19 percent of total), service economy (about 48 percent of total), and manufacturing economy (about 33 percent of total). Individual ETFs exist to track the Morningstar supersector indexes.

Sector ETF Assets Under Management

Given that both Standard & Poor's and the Dow Jones Indexes use similar methodologies for classifying stocks, we'll also proceed with 10 economic sectors for practicality purposes according to research from BlackRock. Of the 10 economic sectors, energy is by far the leading sector as measured by assets under management at $20.3 billion. Technology holds second place at $15.0 billion, while financials earns runner-up props. On the flip side of the coin, telecommunications earns the most irrelevant award with AuM of just under $1 billion. Next closest in line is basic materials with less than $4 billion in AuM.

Economic Cycles and Sector Rotation

Irrespective of the asset class, market segment, or economic sector, market leadership does not continue unabated over time. During certain periods of time, one economic sector will perform strongly, while during other periods of time, other economic sectors will perform strongly. Much of the reason why certain sectors do well or poorly is dependent on a country's place in the economic cycle. When the economy is doing well, then industrials-sector and energy-sector ETFs will perform accordingly. Conversely, when the economy is doing poorly, then utilities and consumer staples are in favor. Furthermore, when an economy is moving from contraction to expansion, technology and consumer discretionary ETFs will get extra attention from retail and institutional investors alike. However, when an economy is transitioning from expansion to contraction, telecommunication and healthcare ETFs will typically outperform the others. Figure 3-3 illustrates this market dynamic.

Sector Risk and Return Profiles

As of early 2011, out of all the sectors, the consumer discretionary sector exhibited the best three-year risk-to-reward trade-off.

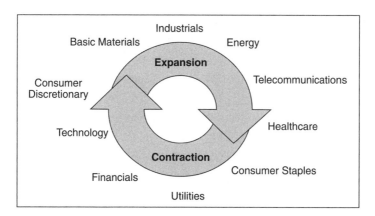

Figure 3-3 **Economic Cycles and Sector Rotation**

Although the consumer staples sector had a modestly higher return, 4.5 percent as compared with 3.2 percent, over the same three-year period, the sector also exhibited higher volatility risk, as measured by standard deviation (the best measure of investment risk). The only two other economic sectors to experience positive performance over the last three years were the technology sector and the basic materials sector. However, no other economic sector exhibited higher volatility risk than basic materials. The financial sector had nearly the same level of risk as basic materials, but also experienced the worst annualized returns (−13.2 percent) by a very wide margin of all sectors. High risk and terrible returns defined financials over the 2008–2010 period. Industrials and the energy sector also had higher than composite levels of risk together with negative annualized returns. The sector with the lowest degree of volatility risk was utilities, but this sector still had a negative return. The data illustrate that it was difficult to generate positive annualized returns over the 2008–2010 period.

FIXED-INCOME ETFs

Given the breadth and depth of the expansive fixed-income market, investors have significant alternatives from which to choose—regardless of whether the investors are seeking current income or if they are attempting to enhance a portfolio from a risk and return trade-off perspective. There are multiple segments within the fixed-income market, from mortgage-backed bonds to corporate bonds and from government bonds to foreign bonds. Each one of these segments exhibits different risk and return potential, which is a favorable situation for investors.

A bond represents a loan to a corporation or to a government entity in order to raise capital to finance many different kinds of expenditures. In many cases, assets of the issuer back each fixed-income security, thus providing the purchaser with some level of protection in the case of default. These assets, or debt instruments, hold the issuer to a contractual obligation to make periodic interest payments to the purchaser on predetermined dates in predetermined amounts until the security reaches maturity or is called by the issuer. Furthermore, the issuer is obligated to repay principal at maturity.

The first fixed-income ETFs that were brought to market were based on U.S Treasuries. Today, the dominant fixed-income ETFs are either actively traded investment-grade bonds or based on broad bond market indexes with significant emphasis on the largest and most creditworthy issuers. Unlike equity ETFs, some fixed-income ETFs do not employ in-kind creation and redemption. Instead, some ETF providers simply issue shares upon delivery of a stated sum of cash, and then purchase the fixed-income securities they require on their own.

Fixed-Income Risk and Return

There is a strong and positive correlation between length of maturity and risk, as Figure 3-4 illustrates. The longer you hold an investment, the longer you are exposed to risk. The longer you are exposed to risk, the greater the probability you can experience partial or total losses. Greater compensation in the form of higher returns is then in order. For those with lower-risk profiles—due to low tolerance, low capacity, or low need—investing in shorter-term

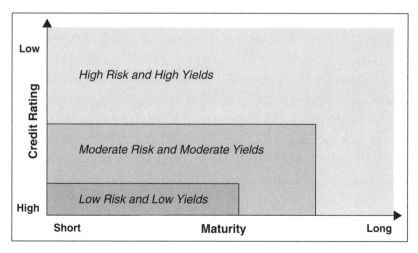

Figure 3-4 **Bond Risk and Yields**

fixed-income investments is prudent. Unfortunately, lower-risk potential is synonymous with lower-return potential.

Yield is the annual rate of return for a fixed-income investment derived from dividing the annual interest payments by the purchase price or market value (depending on when and how you are evaluating the security). Typically, the longer the time to maturity for a fixed-income security, the higher its yield. Thus, short-term securities tend to have lower yields than do long-term securities. This is not always the case, but it tends to hold true the vast majority of the time.

Fixed-Income Market

Fixed-income investments are available in a wide variety of segments. Each segment is different from the next, which is ideal since your goal is to invest in assets that are fundamentally different from one another. Three of the primary factors impacting most investors' decisions when they evaluate fixed-income investments are tax considerations, length of maturity consideration, and credit risk or default risk consideration, which is the uncertainty that an issuer will not be able to make scheduled interest payments or repayments of principal at maturity.

Although bonds are typically issued with a variety of maturities, they can be categorized into one of three segments. These segments include short-term bonds, intermediate-term bonds, and long-term bonds. Short-term bonds have maturities of 1 to 3 years, intermediate-term bonds have maturities anywhere between 4 and 10 years, and long-term bonds have maturities greater than 10 years. Accordingly, long-term bonds tend to have higher yields than intermediate-term bonds, which tend to have higher yields than short-term bonds. (See Figure 3-5 for leading characteristics of bonds.)

Although market values for fixed-income securities are more stable than those for equities and other investments, they do change over time. The primary factors impacting market values include the degree and direction of changing interest rates, fiscal and monetary policies, the macroeconomic health of the national and local

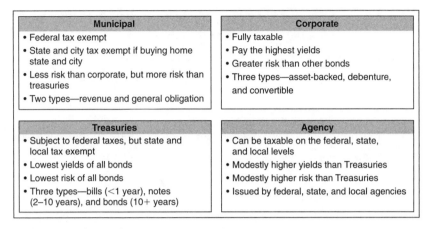

Figure 3-5 **Leading Characteristics of Bonds**

economies, the generic flow of funds into or out of fixed income, and the supply-and-demand balance for specific fixed-income issues.

These are some common fixed-income segments:

- Treasury bills, notes, and bonds
- Municipal bonds
- Agency bonds
- Corporate bonds
- Mortgage-backed securities
- Asset-backed securities
- Banker's acceptances
- Money markets
- Certificates of deposit

Fixed-Income Volatility

Given their greater inherent risk, long-term bonds yield returns that are more volatile than those of both intermediate-term and short-term bonds. Not only are the returns of long-term bonds more volatile, but so are the market values. Fortunately, holding higher-risk, more volatile long-term bonds typically compensates an investor with higher returns over the full holding period.

The same can be said for intermediate-term bonds versus short-term bonds. This is an outstanding example of the golden rule of investing: Risk and return are inescapably linked.

GLOBAL ETFs

Global financial markets have experienced dynamic changes over the last couple of decades. U.S. equities now account for less than half of the total global equity market capitalization. This figure is down from more than two-thirds just a couple of decades ago. As a result, investors who incorporate international assets into their portfolios will find greater opportunities to protect and grow their investments. More specifically, they will improve the risk and return trade-off profile inherent in their portfolio by adding international assets to their asset mix. Consider, for example, two football teams: one with 30 players and one with 100 players. Since only 11 players per team are on the field at any one time, the team with 100 players has a higher chance of finding better players than the team with 30 players, all else being equal. Of course, this is not the case in all situations, but it is so for the vast majority of instances. It is simply the law of numbers. By the way, the numbers 30 and 100 were not selected at random. The number 30 represents the approximate percentage of the total global equity market the U.S. market represents, while the number 100 simply represents the entire global equity market.

Historically, most individual investors have not paid attention to investing globally for three principal reasons:

- Investors have not realized the benefits.
- Transaction costs have been substantial.
- Information for making investment decisions has been unreliable or, worse yet, absent.

Over the years, both transaction costs and availability of information have become more favorable, and many investors have realized the benefits of adding international investments to their portfolios. Adding international assets to an investment portfolio does not come without risk, however. There are new and different risks confronting the global investor. In addition, some risks that a U.S. investor faces are significantly magnified in foreign markets. For example, market liquidity is not as robust in most foreign countries as it is in the United States. Even with that being said, adding international assets to an investment portfolio still has greater potential rewards than potential risks.

Benefits of Global Investing

The ability of investors to reduce portfolio risk is limited in portfolios made up of purely U.S. assets. Investors are able to reduce total risk by minimizing investment-specific risk with U.S.-only assets, but investors cannot reduce systematic risk, or risk attributed to the market and other uncontrollable external factors. When investors add international assets to their portfolios, the market portfolio changes to encompass both the U.S. market and the international market. Thus, reducing market risk is at the heart of global asset allocation.

The reduction of total risk from global asset allocation is driven by the less-than-perfect correlations between U.S. assets and international assets. Asset classes that are not positively correlated with each other perfectly will provide return-enhancing and risk-reducing benefits.

Global correlations are different from country to country; some are highly correlated to U.S. assets, and some are not. Developed countries tend to have higher correlations with U.S. investments and those of emerging market countries due in large part to the significant degree of economic integration. The more interaction among countries, the more influence each country has on the economic conditions of the other. Conversely, the less interaction countries have with each other, the more insulated they are from one another's economic influences—both positive and negative.

No.	ETF	Symbol	Assets ($B)
1	Vanguard MSCI Emerging Markets	VWO	$43.9
2	iShares MSCI EAFE Index	EFA	$36.3
3	iShares MSCI Emerging Markets	EEM	$33.1
4	iShares MSCI Brazil Index	EWZ	$10.0
5	Vanguard MSCI EAFE	VEA	$6.5
6	iShares FTSE China 25 Index Fund	FXI	$6.4
7	Vanguard FTSE All-World ex-US	VEU	$6.1
8	iShares MSCI Japan Index	EWJ	$5.9
9	iShares MSCI Canada Index	EWC	$4.7
10	iShares MSCI South Korea Index	EWY	$3.2

Figure 3-6 **Top 10 Largest International-Category ETFs**

The greatest benefits from adding international assets to a portfolio come from those countries that have the lowest correlations to assets in the United States. However, the governments of many emerging market countries often place harsh regulations and severe restrictions on the investment and repatriation of capital from their countries. Higher potential returns come with higher potential risks. (See Figure 3-6 for a list of the top 10 largest international-category ETFs.)

Global Investing Risks

In aggregate, international investments generally offer higher return potential than do U.S. investments, but they also come with higher risk. Irrespective of the higher risk, international investments are still advantageous because they are not positively correlated with U.S. investments perfectly and thus provide return-enhancing and risk-reducing benefits to one's portfolio. International investments tend to be more risky than U.S. investments for the following major reasons:

- Currency fluctuation risk
- Political risk
- Lack-of-liquidity risk
- Merging-of-asset-correlations risk
- Foreign tax risk

Global Market Structure

The entire investing marketplace begins with the global market portfolio, which comprises all investable opportunities and securities across the world. The global market portfolio can be divided and further subdivided into smaller and smaller markets (see Figure 3-7). For example, the global market portfolio can be divided into developed markets and emerging markets, both of which can be subdivided into various geographic regions. Finally, geographic regions can be subdivided into single-basket countries, each of which constitutes the underlying foundation of the global market structure. Index sponsors, such as MSCI, create indexes based on individual countries, regions, styles, and the broad market. Rights are then sold to ETF providers, who have launched numerous ETFs based on many of the indexes. As a result, investors have excellent ways to gain international investment exposure to geographic areas and markets of their desire.

Country Indexes

As previously mentioned, countries make up the core of the global market portfolio. The most widely recognized indexes tracking individual countries are the MSCI indexes. These indexes capture

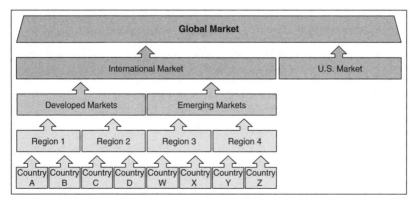

Figure 3-7 **Simplified Global Market Structure**

at least 85 percent of the market capitalization of each country they track. Specifically, MSCI categorizes publicly traded securities into industry groups and then selects stocks from each group to create the country market index. Thus, industry replication is the most important factor in MSCI's methodology.

Regional Indexes

Although there are a number of regional indexes, the two most popular track Europe and Asia Pacific, given their economic weight. As such, MSCI Europe and MSCI Pacific are two of the most widely used indexes by ETF providers. Other regions with investable indexes include the Middle East, Africa, and Latin America. Many of the new regional indexes are divided into developed and emerging markets, such as the emerging Eastern Europe market.

Developed Markets

Developed markets comprise those countries that have stable governments, large economies, robust banking systems, effective legal systems, and, most importantly, strong and liquid investment markets. Countries that meet these provisions typically have a minimum of $20,000 per capita annual gross domestic product (GDP).

Combining the aforementioned MSCI Europe and MSCI Pacific sums to the MSCI EAFE Index, which is the most recognizable index of developed markets. EAFE stands for Europe, Australasia, and the Far East and is composed of approximately 1,000 large-company stocks (slightly over half attributed to Europe) from over 20 developed markets around the globe.

Emerging Markets

Emerging markets are countries where business activity is expanding rapidly. Although there are over 150 countries meeting some classification standard of emerging market status—with over 100 having some resemblance of a stock market—there are only about 40 officially recognized emerging markets in the world, with China and India the largest such markets. MSCI recognizes 21 countries; Standard & Poor's, 19; and Dow Jones, the most: 35.

International Market

The leading index for tracking the international market is the FTSE All-World ex-U.S. Index. This index—appropriately named—tracks all developed and emerging markets around the world with the exception of the United States. Other popular international market indexes include the S&P/Citigroup Primary Market Index (PMI) and the S&P/Citigroup Broad Market Index (BMI).

Global Market

The global market is simply a combination of the international market plus the U.S. market. Dividing the global market portfolio into the two markets provides investors with ways to make targeted investments without overlap. The S&P Global 1200 and S&P Global 100 are two excellent indexes for tracking the global market portfolio. The FTSE All-World Index Series provides solid coverage of the global market as measured by market capitalization.

REAL ASSET ETFs

Real assets, or what are sometimes referred to as alternative investments or hard assets, provide additional ways for you to maximize your portfolio's risk-adjusted return. This asset class goes beyond traditional equities and fixed-income investments; many investors overlook this type of investment. Your investing does not need to be limited to just traditional stocks and bonds. This asset class has been gaining in popularity over the recent few years primarily because ETFs have made real asset investing quicker and easier. More and more investors have been allocating a portion of their portfolios to real assets, namely, real estate and especially commodities, given their unique benefits.

One of the primary reasons underlying the purchase of real assets is to protect your purchasing power—thus a hedge against inflation. Another strong reason investors should consider real assets is because they tend to have very low, and sometimes negative, correlations with equities and bonds. It is for these reasons that including real assets in your portfolio has the potential to enhance returns and reduce investment risk over time. The leading real asset categories for ETF investing include real estate, commodities, and currencies.

Real Estate

Real estate is land, including the air above and the ground below, the permanent buildings or structures attached, and all the natural resources contained within the domain. Real estate is enticing, as it offers low correlations to both equities and fixed income. A properly allocated portfolio should include real estate investments in addition to stocks, bonds, and other investments. This combination of assets has proved to be one of the most effective ways of building a successful portfolio over time. These returns—together with low correlations—are sufficient evidence for building a multiasset-class portfolio that holds real estate.

Investors have two avenues for investing in real estate. First, an investor can buy real estate directly, using capital from his or her investment portfolio, or an investor can invest in real estate investment trusts (REITs). REITs are highly liquid, convenient, well diversified, and offer an ideal way to gain immediate exposure to real estate opportunities. REITs are either privately held or traded on U.S. stock exchanges like common stocks and ETFs. Many REITs hold office buildings, apartments, shopping malls, business centers, industrial buildings, and hotels. The total holdings in REITs still account for only less than 2 percent of the total stock market capitalization.

Directly investing in real estate offers you total control over your investment. Decisions on what leasing terms to use, how much to charge for leases and rents, what discretionary expenses to incur, and when and how to liquidate are squarely at your discretion. However, directly owning real estate is not for everyone. It requires a significant time commitment and unique market knowledge, for starters.

For the vast majority of investors, passively investing in real estate is the preferred and best option—enter REITs. The popularity of REITs has exploded over the last couple of decades due to tax law changes enacted in the early 1990s. According to the National Association of Real Estate Investment Trusts (NAREIT), assets in REITs rose from $7.7 billion in 1985 to over $375 billion only 25 years later in 2010. At the same time, the number of REITs increased from 82 to 153. Furthermore, the total value of all REITs accounts for less than 10 percent of the total investable U.S. real estate.

Under U.S. tax provisions, REITs must distribute at least 90 percent of their earnings to shareholders in the form of dividends or else be subject to corporate taxes on the REIT level. It is for this reason that REITs typically pay strong dividends, a benefit that drives their demand with investors. The market price of REITs typically rises with increases in the inflation rate since REIT income is principally derived from leases and rents, which can be indexed to the inflation rate. In addition, rising inflation can cause stock prices to fall; thus the simple flow of funds out of stocks and into REITs may push up market prices even more.

Commodities

Commodities are the raw materials, hard assets, and tangible products that underscore our civilization in nearly every way possible.

Commodities are the building blocks for virtually everything we eat, everything we use for energy, everything we use in construction, and many of the things we use on a daily basis. Commodities are what gave civilization life from the very beginning with the cultivation of wheat and barley. Moreover, commodities were instrumental in the development of civilization, and we recognize this importance by naming these early periods for them—Copper Age, Bronze Age, and Iron Age.

As a general rule, all commodities are defined by three characteristics, the first being standardization. This means that you can take one unit of a particular commodity and replace it with another unit of the same commodity without issue. Thus, commodities are said to be interchangeable. The second characteristic is tradability, which refers to two distinct features: (1) the existence of a robust marketplace consisting of many buyers and sellers, and (2) the unique futures market, a trading structure not found in traditional investments. The final characteristic is deliverability, which refers to the actual physical exchange of the commodity from the seller to the buyer.

The commodity class called "financials" is the only exception to the rules that commodities must be raw materials and must provide deliverability. For the most part, financials are considered commodities and include indexes, rates, and emissions allowance credits.

Commodity Classes

The global marketplace is vast, with many different commodities. Commodities are classified in one of six major sectors: metals, energy fuels, livestock, agricultural, exotics, and (as noted earlier) financials. Within certain sectors, commodities are further divided into classes such as precious metals and industrial metals:

1. **Precious metals:** Gold, silver, and platinum
2. **Industrial (or base) metals:** Aluminum, copper, lead, nickel, palladium, tin, and zinc

3. **Energies (or energy fuels):** Coal, crude oil, electric power, heating oil, natural gas, unleaded gasoline, and uranium ore
4. **Agriculture (grains and oil seeds):** Corn, soybeans, soybean oil, soybean meal, and wheat
5. **Agriculture (softs):** Cocoa, coffee, cotton, orange juice, and sugar
6. **Livestock:** Feeder cattle, lean hogs, live cattle, and pork bellies
7. **Exotics:** Ethanol, lumber, rubber, and wool
8. **Financials:** Emissions allowance credits, indexes, and rates

Currencies

The foreign exchange market, or forex for short, is a global, worldwide, decentralized, over-the-counter market to facilitate the trading of currencies. Crisscrossing the globe, financial centers serve as anchors of trading among a wide range of different types of buyers and sellers. Transactions are executed around the clock, with the exception of the weekends.

The first currency ETF—introduced in the United States as a grantor trust based on euro deposits—was launched in late 2005 and instantly gave casual investors a quick and easy way to speculate in the currency market. Currency ETFs have gained in popularity for many reasons, most notably to gain or hedge against the fall of the U.S. dollar relative to foreign currencies. Currency ETFs also provide attractive dividends, as the ETF provider takes the assets invested in an ETF and deposits the money denominated in foreign currency with banks to gain interest. Investing in currencies can be a hedge against rising inflation and the subsequent devaluation of the U.S. dollar (or other home country currency, for that matter) against countries with lower rates of inflation. However, currencies can also be used as speculative bets, given fast-moving international turmoil. The U.S. dollar is by far the most actively traded global currency, followed by the euro and then the Japanese yen.

LEVERAGED AND INVERSE ETFs

Some of the newest innovations sweeping the ETF marketplace are leveraged, inverse, and long-short ETFs. The explosion of these types of ETFs is comparable to how traditional ETFs themselves were launched and quickly began to dominate the general investing landscape. Unfortunately, there is much confusion and bad press over these types of ETFs.

Leveraged ETFs have much in common with traditional ETFs but with one major difference: the underlying leverage an ETF provider uses to magnify the performance of the tracking index. Leveraged long, inverse, and long-short ETFs incorporate stocks and bonds just as traditional ETFs do. Up to 85 to 90 percent of their holdings are in securities with which we are familiar. The remaining assets are made up of either derivatives or stocks used as collateral for purposes of generating the desired leverage or inverse capabilities.

Leveraged long and inverse ETFs are available on the most well-known market indexes, including the S&P 500, the Nasdaq–100, and the Dow Jones Industrial Average. Furthermore, nearly all the economic sectors, such as basic materials and financials, and broad-based style and size market indexes are also tracked by leveraged and inverse ETFs. Most of the current leveraged and inverse ETFs in the marketplace today track only market indexes, with little consideration given to proprietary custom indexes. However, leveraged inverse, fixed-income, and commodity funds are less representative of their tracking index. Nonetheless, the mere presence of leverage and inverse capabilities makes these specialty ETFs higher risk and thus not suitable for many investors. So consider the full risk of these ETFs before adding them to your portfolio.

Leveraged long ETFs seek daily investment results, before fees and expenses, that correspond to two to three times ($2\times$ to $3\times$) the daily performance of the underlying tracking index. The two most prominent ETF providers of leveraged and inverse funds are

ProFunds (ProShares) and Direxion. Due to intense SEC scrutiny of leveraged and inverse ETFs, ProFunds and Direxion place a significant emphasis on reinforcing the "daily" performance claim. From time to time, a leveraged or inverse ETF will not properly track its underlying index. There can be significant deviations over the long term, but the returns from day to day are typically much more aligned with the underlying index. The primary reason for purchasing a leveraged ETF is for the higher performance potential over traditional ETFs that track the same underlying index.

While leveraged ETFs magnify the performance of the underlying tracking index (thus providing long equity exposure), inverse ETFs, for all practical purposes, sell short their underlying tracking index (thus providing short equity exposure). Moreover, inverse ETFs can aim for a 1-for-1 inverse price movement, or they can employ leverage like the long leveraged ETFs and produce 2-for-1 (−2×) or 3-for-1 (−3×) inverse price movement of the underlying index. For example, investors have the choice of investing in the ProShares Short S&P 500 (symbol: SH), which aims to generate a 1-for-1 inverse return of the S&P 500, or the ProShares Ultra Short S&P 500 (symbol: SDS), which aims to generate a 2-for-1, or −2×, inverse return of the S&P 500. In doing so, inverse ETFs take even leveraged ETFs to a higher level. Leveraged ETFs and, more importantly, inverse leveraged ETFs are highly volatile and thus are considered two of the most risky types of ETFs in the marketplace.

How They Gain Their Leverage

Leveraged long and inverse ETFs track well-known market indexes. However, in addition to the holdings of the index, these ETFs employ derivatives such as futures contracts and index swaps to generate the leverage or inverse capabilities they desire. Investing in these types of derivatives requires very little cash deposited, and the cash that is used is typically either from dividends and interest income received from the underlying securities or from borrowed cash using the securities in the ETF as loans. The result is a little- to no-cost increase in the market exposure to the underlying securities the ETF is attempting to track. Without the use of derivatives, leverage and inverse capabilities could not exist.

Drawbacks and Disadvantages

Some investors and regulatory agencies do not especially like leveraged long and inverse ETFs. Nevertheless, these types of ETFs do nearly what the ETF provider says they are going to do. That may be at odds with what an investor may have hoped for, given misconceptions before investing. Notwithstanding the debate over the suitability of these specialty funds, there are four drawbacks and disadvantages that investors need to know.

First and foremost, leveraged long and inverse ETFs move upward to three times faster than the pace of market movement. This volatility is disclosed to investors before investment, but the degree of price change still surprises investors. High volatility is high risk, and so investors need to be prepared for the incredible percentage swings these funds may exhibit in any one or more trading sessions.

Second, leveraged long and inverse ETFs have higher expenses than do comparable nonleveraged ETFs. Most of these ETFs charge almost 1 percent expense ratios, which is approaching active-management mutual fund territory.

Third, these specialty ETFs may not do exactly what an investor originally planned. The aim of these ETFs is to generate a return that is two or three times the daily return of the tracking index. The ETF providers make no claims to long-term returns.

Finally, leveraged long and inverse ETFs typically do not offer dividends like those that comparable nonleveraged ETFs might offer. Although the underlying securities pay dividends, the cash is used to finance the purchase of derivatives to generate the desired leverage or inverse capabilities. Nonetheless, most investors do not invest in these types of ETFs for ordinary dividend payments, and so it should not be a significant issue.

In summary, exercise extreme caution and know what you are getting into before using leveraged or inverse ETFs in your portfolio.

CHAPTER 4

The *Perfect* ETF Portfolio

There is no such thing as *one* perfect ETF portfolio for all investors, both retail and institutional alike. The definition of *perfect* is quite different from one investor to another. The same goes for many important things in life, including the perfect job, perfect college, perfect vacation destination, and perfect hobby. Nonetheless, there is something that defines *perfect* in the minds of each person, even if that definition is different from one to another. More specifically, each investor has a good idea of what *perfect* means for his or her own portfolio.

Before we proceed, let's get the obvious out of the way. If you were to ask 100 investors what their definition of the perfect portfolio is, the top response would be something like "the perfect investment portfolio generates abnormally high performance on a consistent basis with, oh yes, little to no fees and tax consequences and immediate liquidity." Of course, that's in the perfect world—a place where we and our portfolios do not reside. So if we are not in a perfect world, then what defines a perfect portfolio? Although the answer is subjective depending on your perspective, there are common characteristics that each perfect portfolio is built upon.

Finally, there is a distinct difference between cause and effect. Having a high-performance portfolio is the effect of specific causes that were incorporated into the portfolio. It is these causes—or characteristics—that this chapter will focus on and not the effects,

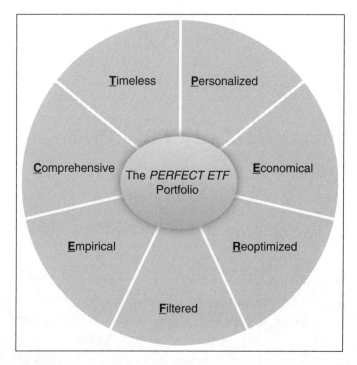

Figure 4-1 **The Perfect ETF Portfolio**

which are much more obvious. After you read the chapter, stop and think about the seven different characteristics. They all are commonsense ideas that each of us can incorporate.

This chapter will illustrate how you as an investor can engineer and sustain a "perfect" portfolio. Figure 4-1 illustrates the seven characteristics that help define exactly what a perfect portfolio looks like and how best to obtain one. We accordingly start with the most important characteristic, personalization.

PERSONALIZE YOUR PORTFOLIO

The most important characteristic for building a perfect ETF portfolio is to personalize it to your unique situation. The four major steps in developing a personalized portfolio include profiling, prioritizing, planning, and positioning.

The first step with building an ETF portfolio is to ensure that it's personalized to each investor's risk profile and financial goals and obligations. The process of personalizing your own portfolio begins with a top-down profile of what is important to you about money and your portfolio. You then need to probe and identify your risk profile, which includes your tolerance for risk, your capacity for risk, and finally your need to assume risk in order to achieve your desired goals. Thereafter you will evaluate your present financial situation, your desired future financial situation, and the gap in between. From here you will prioritize what is necessary to achieve your goals. For instance, do you need to generate high monthly income or do you need to emphasize growth in order to build your wealth as quickly as possible? Your risk profile plays an integral part not only in shaping how you should prioritize your goals but also in planning how to best achieve them.

Once you have identified your risk profile, you then develop an asset allocation mix that conforms optimally to your unique situation. For instance, those investors with a low-risk profile will develop an asset allocation that overweights fixed income, and those investors with high-risk profiles will overweight equities and select real asset classes. Furthermore, depending on your level of income and tax status, overweighting tax-exempt municipal bonds over taxable corporate bonds will increase your tax equivalent yield.

Once you have completed the tasks of profiling, prioritizing, and planning, your job is not finished. You need to position your portfolio for the long term by staying on top of the latest changes in the investing marketplace and investigating and understanding how those changes impact your portfolio. If anything drastically changes in either the investing marketplace or your personal financial situation, then a change in the personalization of your portfolio might be warranted.

The moral of the story: Ensure that you design a customized and tailored portfolio that best matches who you are as a person to who you need to be as an investor and what the aim for your portfolio should be.

MAKE YOUR PORTFOLIO ECONOMICAL

If you are a small business owner, you understand that to increase your cash flow you either have to increase sales or cut expenses. Increasing sales is not entirely easy, or else every small business owner would have a high level of sales. Generating sales is not always within the control of small business owners, but reducing expenses is—far more often. Some expenses can be cut without impacting on operations, while others cannot. The end result of reducing expenses is higher cash flow and increased earnings. The same process works for investment portfolios as well. Although it's far more difficult to increase returns since they are not entirely under our control, investors can reduce portfolio expenses to enhance total net returns.

There are many ways an investor can reduce expenses or otherwise economize his portfolio. Simply employing ETFs instead of mutual funds is one such way. However, the cost difference between ETFs and mutual funds is not as clear-cut as one might initially imagine; there are many variables and variations. Furthermore, not all ETFs are created equal: some have lower expense ratios than do others. Seek out low-cost ETFs whenever and wherever possible, all else being equal.

Another solid way to reduce expenses is to refuse to pay high investment management fees charged by an investment professional if you elect to partner with one. Many brokerage firms and banks push high fees unto unwary investors and attempt to justify them by saying something like, "You get what you pay for." Some firms charge almost 2 percent of the market value of your portfolio per year. Only under unique circumstances should you pay more than 1 percent.

Paying taxes on capital gains can greatly impact performance. As a result, be proactive with tax-management strategies to minimize capital gains or defer them altogether. Selling ETFs with built-up unrealized capital losses can help minimize realized capital gains. Saving a tax dollar here and there can make a big difference with your portfolio over time.

Bid-ask spreads are costs to both buyer and seller. When you purchase an ETF, one-half of the spread paid is a cost to you and the other half is a cost to the seller. Consequently, when you are faced with a situation where the bid-ask spread appears abnormally wide, then placing a limit order somewhere in the spread can help reduce this cost. For example, if you wanted to purchase a certain ETF and at the time of the order the bid-ask spread was $41.00 to $41.30—thus a $0.30 spread—you could attempt to split the spread with a limit order to buy at $41.15. Of course there is no guarantee that your order would fill, but it might, and it would save you money in the process.

Another solid way to reduce total expenses is to seek out firms that charge low trading commissions or commission-free trades altogether on select ETFs. The cost savings from placing purchase and sale orders can add up to a substantial amount over time. TD Ameritrade offers the greatest number of ETFs available for commission-free trading. Other discount firms offer similar free trading but on a lower number of ETFs.

Although annual account fees are not significant, avoiding them can provide cost savings to your portfolio as well. Some brokerage firms charge annual account fees; others charge "inactivity" fees as well if you have not executed trades and generated commission for the firm. In the immortal words of Benjamin Franklin: "A penny saved is a penny earned."

Finally, be smart about the number of trades you place each year. Naturally, the more you trade, the higher your total commissions will typically be. Obviously, if you need to place trades for justifiable investment purposes, then doing so takes precedence over saving a few bucks here and there.

REOPTIMIZE YOUR PORTFOLIO

During the peak of the summer of 2008, the price of West Texas Intermediate (WTI) crude oil rose to $140 per barrel from $60 per barrel in January. However, due to declining economic prospects and worries about where the market might be heading,

WTI fell drastically to a price of about $43 per barrel by the end of that year. If you purchased crude oil at the beginning of 2008 and employed a buy and hold strategy without rebalancing, then you saw your 100-plus percent return from January to July evaporate to a point where you actually lost money over the one-year period. However, if you had taken a more proactive management approach, then you may have either come out ahead with a positive gain or minimized the loss that you would have otherwise experienced if you did not rebalance your portfolio.

The proverbial buy and hold strategy oftentimes turns into a buy and forget strategy—a worrisome situation for you and the health of your portfolio. Buying and selling frequently using market timing and security selection strategies is not the way to go either. If you are an investor in ETFs, it is necessary to first establish an initial allocation for your portfolio based on your risk profile, investment time horizon, and financial goals and objectives. Then you need to engage your portfolio on a set schedule to reoptimize wherever and whenever needed.

Although *reoptimize* is not officially recognized in Merriam-Webster's dictionaries, I use the word extensively since it conveys the exact meaning that I am looking to achieve. Reoptimizing involves four major steps, all beginning with the letter *r* for ease of remembrance. They include reevaluating, rebalancing, relocating, and reallocating.

Reevaluating is the task of examining recent changes in your life and evaluating them within the context of your portfolio. Many things may have changed in your life since you last designed and built your portfolio, and these could impact your financial goals and risk profile. As a result, you should take a long, hard look at your original financial plan and portfolio and make changes where appropriate.

Rebalancing is the task of selling and buying investments to return the current asset class mix to the previously established optimal asset mix. This step involves selling a portion of those asset classes that have become overweight and buying a portion of asset classes that have become underweight.

Relocating is the task of exchanging certain assets for other assets without changing the overall asset mix or the risk and return trade-off profile. Relocating might involve exchanging a corporate bond ETF for a municipal bond ETF to generate more tax-exempt income.

Reallocating is the task of changing the target asset mix within your portfolio given changes in the investing environment or to your personal situation. For example, if you recently received a job promotion to partner as well as a significant increase in compensation, then that would constitute a material reason to increase the risk in your portfolio should you desire to do so. Under this scenario, you might increase your growth allocation by 5 percent and lower your fixed-income allocation by the same amount.

FILTER YOUR PORTFOLIO

Not all indexes and exchange-traded funds are the same; there are differences among the 1,000-plus ETFs available in the marketplace today. You will find many ETFs that track the same market index and others that track obscure market indexes. Furthermore, there are many new ETFs—and the list grows each year—that track totally customizable indexes, which is basically another way to say "active management." Your primary aim is to review and filter the ETFs available in the marketplace to ensure that you have exactly what you need and at a low cost and high tax efficiency. Chapter 7 identifies some of the most important criteria investors should evaluate and use to compare two or more similar ETFs under consideration for inclusion in their own portfolios. Some of these criteria include the category and asset class, expense ratio, index tracked, volatility risk, historical returns, capital gains distributions, unique challenges, and legal structure. There are more criteria presented in Chapter 7 as well.

Once you have identified and included the best-of-breed ETFs in your portfolio, your job is not finished. Investing is a process rather than a one-off event. Over time, providers will introduce new

ETFs to the marketplace, and some of these may be better than the ones you presently have in your portfolio. Your job is to keep an eye out for new ETFs and compare them to what you already own. If the new ETF is better than the one you currently have, then make the swap, all else being equal. In addition, there could be situations where an existing ETF is not performing as you initially expected. Perhaps you were hit with abnormally high capital gains distributions from one of your bond ETFs. An event such as this could cause you to swap the existing ETF for a comparable ETF that is better managed.

In summary, make every effort to filter the ETFs not only before adding them to your portfolio but also when owning them. The reasons you selected them in the first place can change.

BUILD YOUR PORTFOLIO USING EMPIRICAL EVIDENCE

Since investing is not a true science and more of an art form, theory can only take you so far when designing, building, and managing your ETF portfolio. Empirical findings have offered many tools and strategies that investors should use for the best chances of reaching their financial goals. One of the most important empirical findings is the importance and benefits of asset allocation and how the resulting performance edge can provide dividends over time. Rebalancing and reallocating your portfolio have also been shown to provide incremental benefits when utilized as needed. Rebalancing can be accomplished at certain intervals—such as quarterly or annually—or when the asset allocations deviate from predetermined ranges. The choice of which method to use is up to you and/or your investment professional. The important part is to ensure that it gets done. Building out your asset mix with fundamentally different asset classes with low-to-negative correlations has also been shown to lower volatility and enhance risk-adjusted performance over the long term. Many asset classes, such as managed futures and real estate, have low-to-negative correlations with equities, which are typically the bedrock of any ETF portfolio. Be sure you give them the attention they deserve. Another very important finding is the balance investors need to keep between growth-oriented investments (e.g., equities and real assets) and income-oriented investments (e.g., bonds and cash), depending on each investor's length of time horizon. Investors with short-term time horizons should emphasize income-oriented investments, and investors with long-term time horizons should emphasize growth-oriented investments. Finally, empirical findings have shown that long-term bonds exhibit greater price sensitivity to interest rate changes than do comparable short-term bonds. As a result, investors need to structure their portfolios accordingly, depending on their time horizon, income needs, and comfort with volatility.

MAKE YOUR PORTFOLIO COMPREHENSIVE

Building an ETF portfolio for the long term cannot be accomplished with just one, two, or three ETFs. You need to add one or two ETFs per asset class or market segment; anything less will keep your portfolio from achieving the goals you initially established. The most important investment-related decision you need to make is to develop an optimal asset allocation that conforms to who you are as an investor. The second most important task or step is to build out your asset allocation with ETFs. For example, your total equity asset allocation does not call for just one S&P 500 ETF, nor does your total fixed-income allocation require one broad market segment ETF. To exploit the true benefits of asset allocation, you need to gain exposure to multiple asset classes such as U.S. equities and foreign equities. In addition, an efficient portfolio is one that incorporates short-term bonds as well as long-term ones. Yes, you can purchase one ETF that includes both short-term bonds and long-term bonds, but that means that all rebalancing—if it is really executed by the provider—is achieved inside the fund rather than at the shareholder level. Rebalancing is a critical task that should be accomplished by you or your professional investment advisor, not left to the internal workings of an ETF.

A comprehensive ETF portfolio effectively means what it conveys in the name. Do not settle for a basic ETF portfolio or a semi-comprehensive one. The extra work you will need to invest is immaterial compared to the gains you can receive over time. *Comprehensive* means you have exposure to all suitable asset classes with nothing left out of the mix. In my judgment, the more asset classes and market segments you can incorporate, the better. As investors, we do not have the clairvoyance of knowing which asset class will outperform and which will underperform. Thus, we need to include all types and be proactive with reoptimizing our holdings whenever and wherever warranted. Rebalancing allows us to take gains off the table instead of always keeping them at risk in potentially overvalued asset classes or market segments.

When building a comprehensive ETF portfolio, start small and continue to expand big. For example, start with an S&P 500 ETF for your large-cap equity exposure, but begin to transition to an S&P 500 growth and S&P 500 value in the not-so-distant future. The goal is to provide direct exposure to each asset class—which then enhances the benefits of rebalancing—rather than allow them to fluctuate within an ETF and then be subject to ETF internal rebalancing. As you gain more confidence and knowledge of your ETF portfolio, continue to divide broad-based ETFs into their constituent parts. Thus, a broad-based commodity ETF can be replaced with an agriculture ETF, an energy ETF, and a metals ETF. Again, doing so will give you the opportunity to rebalance each ETF as you see fit—and that's a good thing.

MAKE YOUR PORTFOLIO TIMELESS

By this point you have made your asset allocation personalized, economical, and comprehensive, all the while ensuring that your portfolio is filtered, reoptimized, and based on empirical findings. But that's only part of what ensures that your asset allocation creates a perfect portfolio. Why? The reason is that many portfolios are established to do well only when the equity markets are doing well.

Think about that statement for a while. If the stock market were to fall tomorrow, the next week, or the next month, where would your portfolio be? Most likely you would see declines, if not major declines. Do not set yourself up for bad results by establishing an asset allocation that is too dependent on rising equity markets. We all know that markets rise and fall, so incorporating assets into your portfolio that gain only when the equity market advances is self-defeating. If your portfolio has a bias for moving higher only when the stock market rises, then I can guarantee you that there will be times—perhaps more than you had planned—when your portfolio suffers losses, if not insurmountable losses.

Your aim should be to design a "timeless" asset allocation whereby you optimize your portfolio to work in multiple market environments, not just in rising markets. To accomplish this seemingly difficult goal, you need to not only emphasize an asset allocation that can work in multiple markets but also manage your portfolio using tried-and-true management guidelines.

The history of investing is marked by very different events and circumstances that impact portfolios in various ways. We cannot control the uncontrollable (i.e., the market); we can only control how we prepare for the uncontrollable and how we react to uncontrollable events. Therefore, your frame of reference needs to incorporate as much of the history of the market as possible. The market will have many ups and downs, so build a timeless portfolio to deal with any stormy or calm weather.

CHAPTER 5

ETF Risk and Return Fundamentals

With the pursuit of gain comes the risk of loss. Furthermore, for any pursuit of higher gain comes the correspondingly higher risk of loss. Unfortunately, we live in a world where the two go together like peanut butter and jelly. The investing marketplace is fraught with all kinds of risk and all degrees of risk. Although there are numerous benefits to employing ETFs in your portfolio instead of stocks and mutual funds, you cannot escape the basic tenets of investing risk and return. This chapter is all about the basics of risk and return; hopefully, it provides you with a better understanding of investing fundamentals. Although this is now my seventh book on investing, I still hold a strong conviction that investors need to be well grounded in the essentials of investing risk and return before and during the process of managing their portfolios. The concepts in this chapter are more generic in nature, but make no mistake, they apply equally to ETF investing as they do to individual stock, mutual fund, hedge fund, managed futures funds, or any other type of investing approach.

INTRODUCTION TO RISK AND RETURN

No one particularly likes risk, especially when risk translates into portfolio losses like the ones so many of us experienced in 2008 and early 2009. Avoiding or minimizing risk wherever and whenever possible is therefore a top priority. Nevertheless, doing so is not entirely feasible in the world of investing, as there is a clear and profound relationship between risk and return. Risk is an inherent part of any investment undertaking, which makes it critical to understand and manage this inescapable trade-off between risk and return.

Unfortunately, we hear the very opposite thing proclaimed almost every day. We have all seen those crazy infomercials (if you want to call them by that name) that claim reward can be earned with little to no risk. Reward without risk is not possible; if it were, then we would all be millionaires with multiple homes and multiple cars (if that's your thing). Abnormally high returns are not uncommon; however, they are not predictable, nor are they consistent over time. Consequently, if you desire a return that outpaces both inflation and taxes, then you must be prepared to assume some level of risk in your portfolio. You get what you pay for and reap what you sow. Figure 5-1 illustrates the relationship in basic terms between risk and return and the application to portfolio construction.

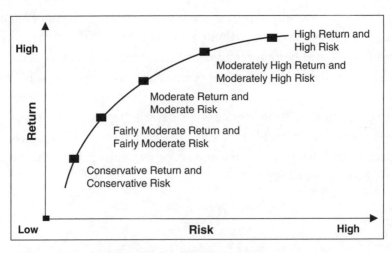

Figure 5-1 **Relationship Between Risk and Return**

Investment return and investment risk and the way they work together are the foundations of asset allocation and its application to building an optimal portfolio. Depending on your objectives and constraints, you may invest in assets that exhibit low risk and therefore the potential for low but stable returns; or you may invest in assets that exhibit high risk and therefore the potential for high but oftentimes volatile returns. In basic asset allocation theory, the higher the potential risk you take, the higher the potential return you should expect to generate over time. Rational investors will not assume a higher level of risk in the hopes of earning a return that a less risky investment will generate.

The trade-off between risk and return is not defined in black-and-white terms. There are multiple shades of gray. As a result, the golden question is how to enhance your returns while minimizing risk. Although risk cannot be entirely eliminated from a portfolio, it can be controlled and managed with a proper asset allocation and diversification policy. Portfolios that are optimally designed, built, and managed will exhibit a higher risk-adjusted return than portfolios that do not subscribe to proper asset allocation policy, regardless of having investments with high potential returns in that portfolio. This is exemplified by modern portfolio theory, which suggests that investors should not evaluate each investment on a stand-alone basis and instead focus on the ability of each investment to enhance the overall risk and return profile of a portfolio. After learning the risk and reward profiles of each asset class, you will then be able to build your own portfolio with an acceptable level of risk and expected return.

The next section of this chapter will discuss investment return, followed by an in-depth discussion of investment risk.

INVESTMENT RETURN

Generating investment return is of primary concern to investors. Why would you invest otherwise? Without appropriate compensation in the form of gains and income, people would not invest their hard-earned money and forgo immediate consumption. Earning the highest return for the least amount of risk assumed is at the core of asset allocation. Investment return can come in many different ways, and it means different things to different people. Although we will be examining quantitative measures of return, do not forget that return can also be expressed in qualitative terms as well, such as emotional comfort, security, and a feeling of independence and control.

It is vitally important that you consider the potential level of return you wish to generate and the level of risk you need to assume in order to obtain that return. Additionally, investing more money in an investment or asset class with higher potential returns does not necessarily mean your return will be any higher than that of someone who invested in an asset class with somewhat lower potential returns. The reason is that it is not the individual investments in your portfolio that are key; rather it is how the component investments work together to form a complete portfolio. For this reason, it is wise to build a portfolio made up of multiple asset classes rather than allocating to only the current asset class or classes with high potential returns. Generally speaking, a higher probability of return also means a higher probability of losing some or all of an investment. Some people are willing to assume that risk, and others are not. This is what makes investing and portfolio construction unique from person to person.

The profit or loss from an investment is composed of both appreciation (or depreciation) in market value over a specific holding period and income (i.e., dividends and interest) received during the same time period. Summing the two profit or loss components and dividing by the market value of the investment at the beginning of the period equals total return. This measure takes into account both the change in the price of the security and any cash flow received during the holding period. It is commonplace in the investment field to measure return using the calculation of total return. An example of calculating total return is as follows.

Suppose you purchase 1,000 shares of JPMorgan Chase common stock at $40 a share. One year later you sell your 1,000 shares at $44 per share. In addition, during your one-year holding period,

Period in Years	Value at End of Holding Period			
	2%	6%	10%	14%
5	$11,041	$13,382	$16,105	$19,254
10	$12,190	$17,908	$25,937	$37,072
20	$14,859	$32,071	$67,275	$137,435
30	$18,114	$57,435	$174,494	$509,502

Figure 5-2 **Growth of a $10,000 Investment**

JPMorgan Chase paid you a $1 per share dividend. Therefore, the total return of your investment, excluding transaction costs and taxes, is 12.5 percent ($4 appreciation plus $1 dividend divided by $40 cost basis). Thus, to calculate total return, one must sum the appreciation (the ending value less the beginning value) and all interest and dividends received during the period and divide by the beginning value.

Even small differences in your rate of return can have big results. Figure 5-2 illustrates how small differences in rates of return can make large differences in the value of an investment over time.

The concept of investment return can be divided into two distinctions: actual return and expected return. Actual return is the return you have generated, whether realized or unrealized, in a past holding period. Expected return is an estimate of what you should generate, both appreciation and income, in a future holding period. Both actual and expected returns are commonly expressed in annualized percentages. Determining actual return is important, since doing so gives you a handle on how well—or poorly—your investments had fared and how best to move forward with any changes such as rebalancing. Similarly, determining expected return is important, as it enables you to fully analyze the profit potential for the level of risk you might take.

The process of forecasting expected returns is a difficult task and typically performed only by very sophisticated and institutional investors. The following are the basic steps for identifying expected return:

1. Forecast all possible material outcomes and scenarios that may occur.
2. Assign probabilities of occurrence to each material outcome.
3. Forecast a return for each specific material outcome.
4. Multiply the probabilities with their related forecasted return.
5. Sum the results (equals the expected return).

Take the following scenario: An analyst estimates that Ford Motor Company has a 25 percent probability of returning 15 percent, a 50 percent probability of returning 10 percent, a 15 percent probability of returning 5 percent, and a 10 percent probability of returning –5 percent. Thus, the expected return is:

$$(0.25 \times 0.15) + (0.50 \times 0.10) + (0.15 \times 0.05) + [0.10 \times (-0.05)] = 9.00 \text{ percent}$$

Identifying potential scenarios and outcomes is typically calculated based on estimates of how well the economy and other macroeconomic factors will perform during the holding period under consideration. The resulting expected return is simply an estimate, given each economic scenario possible. Monte Carlo computer simulations are sometimes used to help refine potential results. All this is done to give investors a better idea of investment risk and thus allow them to make more informed decisions.

INVESTMENT RISK

Investment risk can be defined in several different ways, as one investor views risk differently from another. Some investors define *risk* as losing money, while others define it as being unfamiliar—and therefore uncomfortable—with an investment. Still others define *risk* as contrarian risk, or the risk that investors feel when they are not "following the crowd." Although all the aforementioned definitions of the term are sound, *risk* is best defined as the uncertainty that actual investment returns will match expected returns. For example, pension funds and insurance companies view risk as the uncertainty that they can meet future benefit obligations.

The uncertainty of meeting future commitments and funding obligations is a sensible and objective way to view portfolio and investment risk. Future commitments and funding obligations can include paying for college, buying a vacation home, starting a business, or just supplementing social security to pay for living expenses in the golden years.

Taking this concept of risk further, gaps between actual and expected returns can be attributed to volatility of returns over a specific time period. Greater monthly price movement of a particular security—regardless of direction—equates to a higher volatility measure. Higher volatility is considered higher risk, while lower volatility—and therefore more stable prices—is considered lower risk for an investment. Volatility also impacts total performance. Portfolios with greater volatility over multiple periods during one holding period will exhibit lower long-term compounded growth rates of return than portfolios with lower volatility over multiple periods during the same holding period. This is often referred to as the "sequence of returns." Thus, it is essential to minimize volatility in your portfolio for maximum performance over time.

Risk management and proper asset allocation help control both the frequency and the amount of portfolio losses over time. Since you rely on estimates of future returns to design your optimal portfolio, it is critically important that actual returns come close to matching expected ones. Investments with more predictable returns are thus considered lower risk and more favorable for most investors. Conversely, investments with less predictable returns are considered higher risk and typically less favorable for most investors.

Sources of Investment Risk

There are two primary sources of investment risk. The first is called "systematic risk," or the risk attributed to relatively uncontrollable external factors; the second is called "unsystematic risk," or the risk attributed directly to the underlying investment. Let's look at systematic risk first.

Systematic Risk

Systematic risk results from conditions, events, and trends occurring outside the scope of the investment. There are four primary types of systematic risk: exchange rate risk, interest rate risk, market risk, and purchasing power risk. At any one point, there are different degrees of each risk occurring. These risks will cause the demand for a particular investment to rise or fall, thus impacting returns:

1. **Exchange rate risk:** The risk that the value of an investment will be impacted by changes in the foreign currency market. For example, if you live in the United States and own a foreign asset, then changes in the value of that foreign currency relative to the U.S. dollar will impact your return. If the U.S. dollar increases in value, then your return declines, since it will take more foreign currency to buy one U.S. dollar. Conversely, a declining U.S. dollar will increase your return, all else being equal.

2. **Interest rate risk:** The risk attributed to the loss in market value for both fixed-income and equity securities due to a change in the general level of interest rates. For bonds and other fixed-income securities, rising interest rates can negatively impact market values. Why? Primarily because as interest rates rise, the availability of more attractive investments with higher yields also

increases. For example, if you owned a bond yielding 5 percent and interest rates increased by 1 percent to 6 percent, then the demand for 6 percent bonds will grow and the demand for 5 percent bonds will fall. This translates to lower market values for your 5 percent bond. For equities, changes in interest rates can impact business operations, such as the number of mortgage originations for banks and the number of new-home starts for home builders.

3. **Market risk:** The risk attributed to the loss in market value for individual investments because of price declines in the entire market portfolio. When the overall market falls, then most—but not all—investments decline in sympathy with the overall market. Consider the "flash crash" of 2010, for example. Although that case is an extreme one, few stocks were up when the Dow Jones Industrial Average was down close to 1,000 points at one time in the day. If you had planned to sell your investment on that day, you were not very happy.

4. **Purchasing power risk:** The risk attributed to inflation and the resulting rising prices that erode the real value of an investment over time. This means that $100 today will buy less one or more years into the future. When prices for goods and services are rising faster than expected, then your ability to sustain your current lifestyle into retirement will be more challenging.

Unsystematic Risk

Unlike systematic risk, unsystematic risk is not attributed to external factors. This source of risk is unique to an investment, such as the debt level of a particular company, the soundness of a company's management team, and the industry in which a company operates.

The principal types of unsystematic risk include, but are not limited to, the following:

1. **Business risk:** The risk attributed to a company's operations, particularly those involving sales and income. For example, persistent declining sales for a specific company can mean the loss of investor confidence followed by a declining stock price.

2. **Financial risk:** The risk attributed to a company's financial stability and structure, namely the company's use of debt to leverage earnings. Companies with more debt have higher principal and interest payments, which is not a major concern during good times. However, during bad times, satisfying higher debt payments can be a significant challenge. As a result, companies with more debt than others are considered to be more risky.

3. **Industry risk:** The risk attributed to a group of similar companies within a particular industry or sector. Investments tend to rise and fall based on what peer companies are doing. A big downside movement in price for one company stock will typically bode poorly for other stocks in that same peer group.

4. **Liquidity risk:** The risk that an investment cannot be purchased or sold at a price at or near market prices. The more liquid an investment, the easier it is to buy or sell at current market prices. Illiquidity can cause you to sell at a much lower price than originally expected.

5. **Call risk:** The risk attributed to an event where an investment may be called (i.e., forced to sell back to the issuer) prior to maturity. This may leave the investor unable to reinvest the proceeds at the same or a higher interest rate. This risk is associated with fixed-income securities.

6. **Regulation risk:** The risk that new laws and regulations will negatively impact the market value of an investment. For example, a state government may pass a law

requiring manufacturers to add new and costly pollution control systems in their factories. Irrespective of the environmental benefits, adding costly systems could harm a company's financial position, subsequently making it less attractive to investors.

Summing systematic and unsystematic risk equals total risk. Since the goal of asset allocation is to create a well-diversified portfolio, unsystematic risk is considered less important because it can—and should—be eliminated with proper diversification. Therefore, an optimal portfolio should possess only systematic risk, or risk resulting from market and other uncontrollable external factors.

Measuring Investment Risk

Different investments have both different types of risk and different degrees of risk. So it is essential to quantify risk in order to make comparisons across the broad range of asset classes for better decisions. As mentioned previously, risk is best defined as the uncertainty that actual returns will not match expected returns. Intuitively, one can see that the greater the difference between actual and expected returns for an investment, the less predictable and uncertain that investment is considered to be. This translates into greater risk for investors.

Using historical return data, we are able to measure risk. Historical volatility data can be obtained using numerous intervals of time—days, weeks, months, and years—with monthly volatility generally used in practice. In simple analysis, averaging the degrees of difference between actual and expected returns for a specific investment gives us the statistical measure called "standard deviation." Although we will not get into the technical specifics of how to calculate it, standard deviation is a statistical measure of the degree to which actual returns are spread around the mean actual return. Expressed as a percentage, standard deviation is considered the best—but not the sole—measure of risk. A higher standard deviation means higher risk, and a lower standard deviation means lower risk. Unfortunately, the job is not finished with calculation of the standard deviation. Since the price for any security changes over time, so to do standard deviations; they are not static. Some asset classes will change more frequently and to a greater degree than do other asset classes.

Volatility typically rises during periods of declining prices and moderates during periods of advancing prices. Historically speaking, even though the volatility of asset classes may change in the short term, volatility ranges have remained relatively stable over the long term. That is good news for investment planning, since we are dealing with more predictable inputs.

Because actual returns are impacted by both systematic and unsystematic risks, standard deviation is a measure of total risk. As a result, standard deviation gives an investor a way to evaluate both the risk and return elements of an individual investment. Although standard deviation is one of the best measures of risk, it is not without issues—not by far. For example, standard deviation may vary from analysis to analysis, depending on the holding period (in years) selected for comparison. Due to many factors, it is best to utilize a standard deviation that is derived from actual returns from the last 10 to 20 years. Using returns older than 20 years may result in incorporating risks in the investment that are no longer present or that were not in place over 20 years ago. For example, 40 years ago tobacco companies were not inundated with class-action lawsuits regarding the health concerns of smoking. Today these class-action lawsuits can have a significant impact on the companies' stock prices. Consequently, using data collected from recent periods is more appropriate to calculate standard deviation.

Another measure of risk in common use—and one much easier to calculate—is called "beta," a number expressed in absolute terms rather than as a percentage. A beta of above 1.0 is considered more volatile than the market, whereas a beta of less than

1.0 is considered less volatile than the overall market. Lastly, betas of 1.0 move in sync with the overall market. Thus, if an investment has a beta of 1.5, then that investment on average will be 50 percent more volatile than the overall market; an investment with a beta of 0.75 will be 25 percent less volatile on average than the overall market.

> **Example:** Stock A has a beta of 1.2. Thus, if the S&P 500 is expected to rise by 5 percent during the holding period, then Stock A is expected to rise by 6 percent (5 percent multiplied by 1.2). Conversely, if the S&P 500 is expected to fall by 5 percent during the holding period, then Stock A is expected to fall by 6 percent.

As you can see from the example just given, when the market is rising, higher beta investments generally earn higher returns than the overall market. Conversely, when the market is declining, these same investments generally have lower returns than the overall market, not including dividends.

Although beta is easier to understand, calculate, and apply than standard deviation, it too has drawbacks. The most significant one is that beta is not representative of total risk. Beta is derived from the volatility of a given investment relative to the overall market. Thus, beta measures only systematic or market risk, not unsystematic risk. Remember, however, that a properly built portfolio will have minimal unsystematic risk since it should be diversified away.

In practice, investors desiring market rates of return can generally obtain them by investing in securities with betas of 1.0. Moreover, investors desiring to be more aggressive can potentially obtain higher returns by investing in securities with betas higher than 1.0. Of course, securities with betas above 1.0 have more inherent risk. Figure 5-3 shows some actual standard deviations and betas.

ETF	Symbol	Standard Deviation	Beta
Consumer Discretionary Sector SPDR	XLY	23.0	1.12
Consumer Staples Sector SPDR	XLP	12.4	0.58
Energy Sector SPDR	XLE	25.1	1.12
Financial Sector SPDR	XLF	33.5	1.61
Health Care Sector SPDR	XLV	15.7	0.63
Industrial Sector SPDR	XLI	26.2	1.33
Materials Sector SPDR	XLB	27.7	1.36
Technology Sector SPDR	XLK	18.6	0.90
Utilities Sector SPDR	XLU	12.6	0.43
SPDR S&P 500	SPY	18.9	0.99

Figure 5-3 **Actual Standard Deviations and Betas**

Volatility Creates Uncertainty

The following charts illustrate why volatility is used as a measure of risk. Figure 5-4 presents two exchange-traded funds with the same 10 percent expected return per year but with different degrees of price volatility. ETF A has a lower degree of price volatility, and ETF B has a higher one.

As you can see from Figure 5-4, the price of ETF A is expected to fall within a tighter range after one year than the price for ETF B over the same time period. Thus, ETF B is expected to exhibit a greater degree of price volatility than ETF A. Now, assume that you are an investor who is trying to determine which ETF has the higher probability of achieving a 9 percent return over the one-year period. This can be achieved through simple math by taking 100 percent minus the desired return less the lowest expected return for the year divided by the expected range of returns for each ETF. For simplicity, the following example does not take into consideration the concept of the bell curve:

$$\text{ETF A} = 100\% - \frac{(9\% - 8\%)}{(12\% - 8\%)} = 75\% \text{ probability}$$

$$\text{ETF B} = 100\% - \frac{(9\% - 6\%)}{(14\% - 8\%)} = 63\% \text{ probability}$$

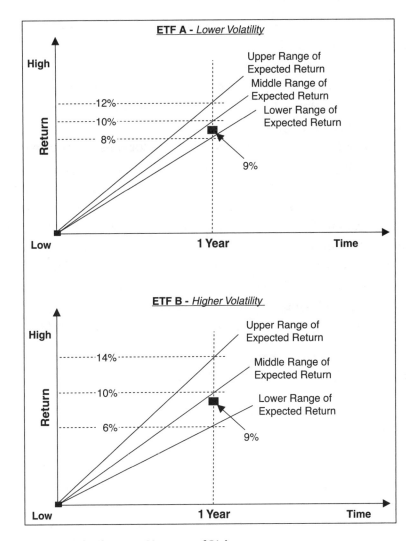

Figure 5-4 **Volatility as a Measure of Risk**

RISK AND RETURN TRADE-OFF

Given the direct relationship between risk and return, investors are able to measure this relationship to build a portfolio with the appropriate risk and return trade-off profile. By using what is called the Sharpe ratio, or simply dividing the "excess expected return" of an investment by its standard deviation (level of risk), we are able to ascertain the amount of excess expected return per unit of risk for any investment, including ETFs. Doing so helps us compare, contrast, and select investments with dissimilar expected returns and levels of risk. Excess expected return is defined as the expected return minus the risk-free rate, or the rate you can earn from investing in U.S. Treasury bills.

Suppose you are evaluating two ETFs for possible investment: ETF A and ETF B. ETF A has a standard deviation of 25 percent and an excess expected return of 8 percent over the proposed holding period. By dividing the excess expected return of 8 percent by the standard deviation of 25 percent, we find that ETF A has a risk and return trade-off profile of 0.32. Similarly, ETF B has a standard deviation of 15 percent and an excess expected return of 6 percent. This translates into a risk and return trade-off profile of 0.40. As you can see, although ETF A has the higher expected return, it does not provide the highest level of expected return per unit of risk—that prize goes to ETF B.

RISK AND RETURN RELATIONSHIP

Investors who take greater risk should be compensated with greater potential return. Depending on your risk profile, the more risk you assume, the higher your expected return. Of course, there are exceptions to the rules—aren't there always? To better understand this relationship between risk and expected return, a model called the "efficient frontier" has been developed. The efficient frontier—illustrated by an upward-sloping curved line—represents the investments with the highest risk and return trade-off profiles, or those investments with the highest expected returns for a specific level or unit of risk.

As you can see from Figure 5-5, by moving up the efficient frontier, investments present a greater potential for return, but they also come with greater risk. Nevertheless, each point on the efficient frontier exhibits the highest expected total rate of return for the level of risk exhibited. There will be many investments available and plotted on the graph, but only those with the best risk and return trade-off profiles will appear on the efficient frontier.

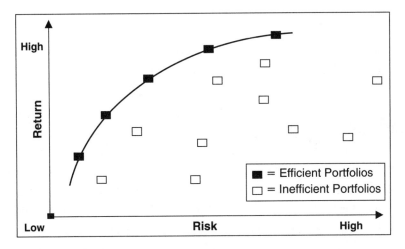

Figure 5-5 **Hypothetical Efficient Frontier**

Your objective is to select investments somewhere along the efficient frontier according to your risk and return trade-off profile. Some investors will place their investments near the top of the slope, while others with lower risk and return trade-off profiles will place their investments on a lower part of the slope to the lower left.

Regardless of whether your portfolio is an 80/20, 70/30, 60/40, or 50/50 equity to fixed income, as long as each portfolio combination exhibits the highest expected total rate of return for a given level of risk, then it will be plotted somewhere along the efficient frontier. Portfolios that do not exhibit the highest expected total rates of return per unit of risk will be plotted below the slope of the efficient frontier, and that means a suboptimal or inefficient portfolio.

Understanding this relationship between risk and return is critical, as it underlies the process of allocating assets. Without a true understanding of this relationship, you may design a portfolio that either exhibits greater risk than desired or generates lower actual returns given the inclusion of less risky assets. As we will see in the next chapter, the process of asset allocation involves estimating expected returns for each asset class and then determining, within the context of your risk and return trade-off profile, what percentage of the portfolio should be allocated to each asset class.

ASSET CLASSES AND RISK

Different asset classes possess different types and different amounts of risk, including different expected returns. Each type of risk is derived from one or more sources of risk. Regardless of the type and source of investment risk, asset allocation will allow you to control and manage your risk exposure to the best of your advantage.

As previously mentioned, it is simply not enough to focus on the merits of one particular asset class, as it is how each asset class moves in relation to the other asset classes that truly matters. Regardless of the risk and return potential for each asset class, keep in mind that understanding the asset class's fundamentals and how they impact a portfolio is most important. Figure 5-6 illustrates this all-important lesson.

TEN RULES FOR PORTFOLIO RISK REDUCTION

Risk, and the endeavor to control, reduce, or eliminate it, is as old as the financial markets themselves. Regardless of the new technology, the new hot products, or the new financial models, successful investing is all about maximizing the inescapable trade-off between risk

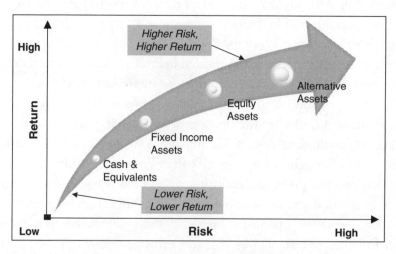

Figure 5-6 **Asset Class Risk and Return Trade-Off Profiles**

and return. The following is a list of 10 reasonable rules you may want to consider for reducing the level of risk in your portfolio:

1. **Understand your risk:** Knowing your level of portfolio risk will enable you to make better and more informed decisions. Remember that *risk* is best defined as uncertainty that actual returns will match expected returns.

2. **Build a multi-asset-class portfolio:** Holding multiple asset classes will smooth the volatility risk you would otherwise experience from holding only a minimal number of asset classes.

3. **Target low correlations:** Low correlations among asset classes further smooth out volatility risk since lower correlations mean that the prices for two asset classes do not move in tandem with each other.

4. **Add fundamentally different asset classes:** Asset classes that are fundamentally different exhibit return-enhancement and risk-reduction potential. Hold a combination of these asset classes wherever feasible.

5. **Diversify each asset class:** Diversification is not the same as asset allocation. Diversify each asset class to reduce unsystematic risk, or investment-specific risk unique to single asset classes or investments.

6. **Rebalance your portfolio:** Your portfolio asset mix will change over time as the values of your investments change. To keep this added risk in check, rebalancing back to your original allocations should be done on a frequent basis—at least annually, but better yet, quarterly.

7. **Use common sense:** When selecting the suitable level of risk for your portfolio, it is more important to be approximately correct than to be precisely wrong.

8. **Hedge risk:** Although not for all investors, hedging risk with options, swaps, futures, and position-neutralizing short sales can protect against severe market declines.

9. **Exercise discipline:** Employing a steadfast approach will outperform a constantly changing approach any day of the week.

10. **Consider assistance:** Risk is best managed by experienced people, not financial models. Professional help may provide you with the resources and comfort you need.

CHAPTER 6

Designing, Building, and Managing ETF Portfolios

This chapter is dedicated to the self-directed investor for designing, building, and managing a portfolio of exchange-traded funds. Actually, many of the topics are applicable to non-ETF portfolios as well, but they are deliberately tailored here with ETFs in mind. The first part of this chapter begins with an essential lesson in asset allocation and its critical importance to building portfolios. This is followed up by a detailed discussion of the investor-centric and investment-centric input factors that determine what a personalized asset allocation looks like. The last two sections discuss how to build and manage your ETF portfolio for long-term success.

IMPORTANCE OF ASSET ALLOCATION

Numerous landmark research studies have concluded that *how* you allocate your assets, rather than *which* individual investments you select or *when* you buy or sell them, is the leading determinant of investment performance over time. Not stock picking, or market timing, or the latest and greatest hot investment without risk is the leading determinant of investment performance over time.

No book on exchange-traded funds would be complete without a solid grounding in asset allocation. As we saw with the preceding chapter, the relationship between risk and return is central to the investing decision framework. This relationship essentially implies that to earn higher levels of return, investors need to assume higher levels of risk. There is simply no other way to accomplish this aim. In addition, investors seeking to assume lower levels of risk will typically earn lower rates of return. Asset allocation is very much related to risk and return and the relationship they play in portfolio construction. Investing in exchange-traded funds should not be approached as a stand-alone, single investment. Rather, it should be seen as part of the overall picture—a way to enhance and build out asset allocation. For a thorough discussion of asset allocation, please pick up a copy of *Understanding Asset Allocation* (Frush, McGraw-Hill, New York, 2006).

Asset allocation is best described as the way you optimally divide your investment portfolio and other investable money into different asset classes for maximum benefit. The concept underlying this allocation method is that you will reduce portfolio risk and enhance your long-term risk-adjusted return. In other words, asset allocation provides you with your best opportunity to earn solid returns over time while assuming the level of portfolio risk most suitable for your unique situation. The allocation of your assets is based on a number of very important factors, such as current financial position, investment time horizon, level of wealth, financial needs and goals, and risk profile. There are a few other minor factors as well, which are discussed at length later in this chapter.

The three most important inputs that determine your asset allocation are your financial objectives and obligations, your investment time horizon, and your risk profile. For building an optimal portfolio, your unique risk profile is of utmost importance. Your risk profile includes three components: your tolerance for risk, your capacity for risk, and your need to assume risk. Much like an army that moves only as fast as its slowest unit, portfolios should be constructed according to the least common denominator for risk of the three components that constitute risk profile.

Al-Location, Al-Location, Al-Location

One of the leading adages of classic wisdom most synonymous with business success is "location, location, location." Nearly everyone has heard this expression because it is so very true. Building a successful portfolio is not very different from building a successful business. This same classic wisdom that applies to business success applies to investment success as well, but it is expressed with a twist: "Al-location, al-location, al-location." Location, or "al-location" with investing, can mean the difference between success and failure. Before selecting a location, successful business owners do their homework; they do not make ad hoc decisions. As an investor, you should approach your investing in the same manner.

Asset Allocation Analogy

To better help illustrate the significant benefits of asset allocation, let's consider an analogy to hockey. Employing asset allocation is like a hockey player choosing to wear protective equipment: helmet, shoulder pads, hip pads, kneepads, and so on. If the hockey player were to take off his protective equipment, he could probably skate faster, cut easier, and pass the puck better. As a result, he could become a dominant player. But it doesn't take a rocket scientist to recognize that by not wearing the proper hockey protective equipment, he is being very unwise and foolish. One hit into the boards from an opponent and he could be out of the game for a very long time, if not forever. No more domination.

Employing proper asset allocation works much the same way. An investor who does not wear proper "protective equipment" (i.e., have a well-allocated and diversified portfolio) may experience uncommonly superior returns for a short period of time; however, eventually she will take a devastating hit that might crash a portfolio, possibly severely enough that it won't recover. Taking a serious hit may not happen right away, but it will happen at some point. Think of the dot-com bubble burst in the early 2000s and the financial crisis crash of 2008.

Foundation of Asset Allocation

Asset allocation is founded on two celebrated and highly influential investment theories. These two are the modern portfolio theory (MPT) and the efficient market hypothesis (EMH), which is essentially a refinement of MPT. These two theories are the most discussed and most widely used theories in all investment management.

Modern portfolio theory says that investors and portfolio managers should not evaluate each investment on a stand-alone basis. Rather, each investment should be evaluated based on its ability to enhance the overall risk and return profile of a portfolio. For instance, according to MPT, when faced with two investments with identical expected returns but different levels of risk, investors should select the investment that has the lower risk. Said another way, a rational investor should select the investment with the higher expected return when faced with two investments that have different expected returns but identical levels of risk.

As you can see from Figure 6-1, when faced with investments A and B, a rational investor will select investment B over investment A because the total return of investment B is higher, with both having the same level of risk. Moreover, when faced with investments B and C, a rational investor will select investment C over investment B because the total risk of investment C is lower, with both having the same total return. This is rather simple stuff, but it was revolutionary when first put forth.

Additionally, MPT introduces the concept of correlation and stresses how it enhances the risk and return profile of a portfolio. The Employee Retirement Income Security Act of 1974, which governs the management of pension funds, emphasizes this point,

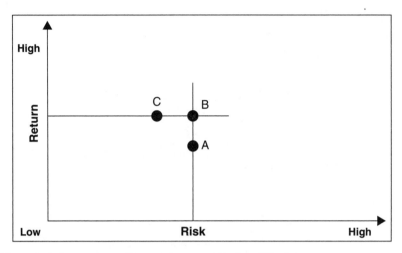

Figure 6-1 **Investment Alternatives and Rational Decisions**

thus essentially endorsing MPT. Harry M. Markowitz, who was awarded the Nobel Prize in Economics in 1990, is considered the "father of modern portfolio theory" for this work.

Finally, the efficient market hypothesis asserts that capital markets are "informationally efficient," meaning one cannot achieve excess risk-adjusted returns consistently over time since the information relied upon to make such a decision is publicly available at the time the investment is made.

Empirical Findings

Authors Gary P. Brinson, L. Randolph Hood, and Gilbert L. Beebower, in the landmark research study "Determinants of Portfolio Performance" published in the *Financial Analysts Journal* (July–August 1986, pp. 39–44), concluded that asset allocation policy is by far the principal determinant of investment performance over time. The researchers discovered that, contrary to popular belief at the time, security selection and market timing determined only a small part of investment performance over time. As you can see from Figure 6-2, asset allocation policy explained 93.6 percent of investment performance, while security selection, market timing,

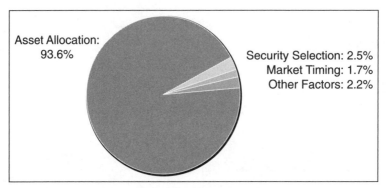

Figure 6-2 **Determinants of Investment Performance**

and other factors (including costs) explained 2.5 percent, 1.7 percent, and 2.2 percent of investment performance, respectively.

Gary Brinson, Gilbert Beebower, and Brian D. Singer used updated information to conduct a follow-up study. Titled "Determinants of Portfolio Performance II: An Update," published in the *Financial Analysts Journal* (May–June 1991, pp. 40–48), this study arrived at nearly the same conclusion as the previous study. As such, the subsequent study concluded that asset allocation policy is the primary factor explaining investment performance over time. Again, the second study found that security selection and market timing explained only a fraction of investment performance.

As you can see from Figure 6-3, asset allocation policy was found to explain 91.5 percent of investment performance, while security selection, market timing, and other factors explained 4.6 percent, 1.8 percent, and 2.1 percent of investment performance, respectively.

In yet another significant research study, renowned practitioners Roger G. Ibbotson and Paul D. Kaplan concluded in their study titled "Does Asset Allocation Policy Explain 40, 90, or 100 Percent of Performance?" published in the *Financial Analysts Journal* (January–February 2000, pp. 26–33) that asset allocation policy explains about 90 percent of investment performance over time.

If security selection and market timing do not play a significant role in determining investment performance over time, a good question to investigate is whether or not individual industries play

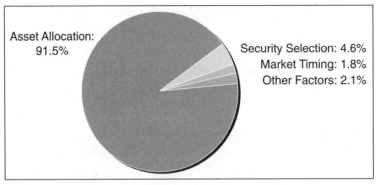

Figure 6-3 **Determinants of Investment Performance II**

a role. According to Eugene F. Fama and Kenneth R. French, they generally do not. In their research paper "Industry Costs of Equity," published in the *Journal of Financial Economics* (February 1997, pp. 153–193), the researchers concluded that although specific industries can influence market prices, they do so only in a random and short-term way.

Asset-Class Behavior

During certain time periods some asset classes will perform well, whereas during other time periods other asset classes will perform well. Unfortunately, we do not know which asset class will perform well during any specific period, and therefore it is vitally important to be invested in multiple asset classes at all times. The benefits of asset allocation and diversification are received when you invest in multiple asset classes where there is a fundamental difference among them. The principal benefit is to enhance the risk-adjusted return of your portfolio. This is referred to as the "allocation effect." Allocating to multiple asset classes does not necessarily guarantee consistently higher returns with corresponding low levels of risk. That simply cannot be accomplished consistently over time. During certain periods, your portfolio will experience strong asset allocation benefits, while during other times your portfolio will have subdued asset allocation benefits.

Determining your optimal asset allocation comprising multiple asset classes requires a solid understanding of some very important points. First, there is no perfect allocation or perfect plan. There are only good to very good plans that will help you achieve your goals. Second, make sure to learn the key specifics of each asset class, such as general correlations, historical returns, and typical risk levels. Third, understand that forecasting future correlations, returns, risk levels, and price movements—although important—is an extremely difficult endeavor. Leave those tasks to the experts whenever possible. Fourth, a portfolio with a higher number of asset classes is more advantageous than a portfolio with fewer asset classes. Last, remember to build a portfolio with an asset allocation that complements your unique situation.

In Figure 6-4, A represents a hypothetical portfolio of large-cap stocks; B represents a hypothetical portfolio of large-cap stocks and small-cap value stocks; C represents a hypothetical portfolio of large-cap stocks, small-cap value stocks, and corporate bonds; D represents a hypothetical portfolio of large-cap stocks, small-cap value stocks, corporate bonds, and real estate; and E represents a hypothetical portfolio of large-cap stocks, small-cap value stocks, corporate bonds, real estate, and international stocks.

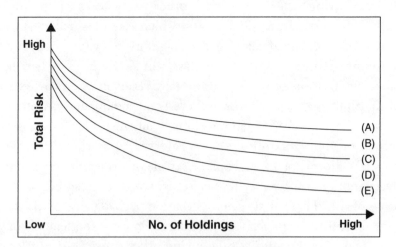

Figure 6-4 **Advantage of Multi-Asset-Class Portfolios**

DESIGNING AN ETF PORTFOLIO

Designing an ETF portfolio is all about establishing your optimal asset allocation. This may seem simple enough, but it's more difficult than it appears. Depending on your risk profile and financial constraints and obligations, you may employ a 60/40 or 70/30 allocation of equity to fixed income. However, your situation might lend itself to a much more aggressive allocation—perhaps an 80/20 split. Once you have identified an optimal asset mix, you must then decide whether or not you will build a basic portfolio—which will include the major asset classes only—or you will pursue a sophisticated portfolio thereby including many more asset classes (e.g., such as global real estate, precious metals, and both value and growth styles). Irrespective of which allocation mix you select, it needs to reflect what you are looking to achieve with your investing, as each asset class has a purpose and unique style. Seeking out the help from a qualified investment professional can pay extra dividends (maybe even literally) with this task. The sample ETF portfolios provided in Chapter 9 and asset allocation questionnaire in Appendix B can provide some assistance and perspective on how involved this activity should be.

When determining the best asset mix, you need to consider a number of factors. These factors can be classified as either investor-centric inputs or investment-centric inputs. The investor-centric inputs are based on your own attitudes, personal financial position, and investing needs and goals. Investment-centric inputs, on the other hand, are not directly related to you and arise directly from the market and other uncontrollable factors such as correlations and volatility risk. The following is a discussion of the factors divided into the investor-centric inputs first, with the investment-centric inputs thereafter.

Investor-centric Factors

This section examines specific factors attributed to individual investors that in aggregate impact—along with investment-centric factors—the asset allocation decision and the resulting asset mix of investments.

Risk Profile

Along with your time horizon, your risk profile is perhaps the most important input to the asset allocation decision. Your risk profile is made up of three similar yet separate components. These components are your tolerance for risk, your capacity for risk, and your need for risk. The lowest measure of the three is considered the maximum level of risk you should assume in your portfolio. For example, although an investor may have a high tolerance for risk and high capacity to assume it, that investor may not have the need to assume risk. Why? Many investors have a level of wealth that is more than adequate to fund their lifestyle and goals, now and in the future. Unfortunately, investor risk profile is difficult to measure for three reasons. First, risk is specific to a situation and not a general rule applicable to all situations. Second, risk is not easily understood, and people therefore act irrationally and unpredictably. Third, an investor's risk profile changes over time; it is not static.

Determining your risk profile is rather subjective and therefore difficult to express as a quantifiable factor. One good solution is to complete a risk profile questionnaire available from most financial services firms.

SMART Goals

Having investment goals and striving to attain those goals will give your investing purpose. Goals will directly impact your asset mix. Do you need money for a new home, or will you be purchasing a new business perhaps? As a result, you may want to overweight fixed income and underweight equities. Conversely, overweighting equities is ideal for the parents saving for a future college education over 10 years away. Matching asset classes to goals is key to achieving long-term investment success. The word *SMART* is oftentimes used to illustrate the five characteristics of well-designed goals:

- **Specific:** Your goals should be unambiguous, clear, and well defined.

- **<u>M</u>easurable:** Your goals should be quantifiable and trackable.
- **<u>A</u>ccepted:** Your goals should be acknowledged and motivational.
- **<u>R</u>ealistic:** Your goals should be achievable and attainable, but not lofty.
- **<u>T</u>imely:** Your goals should be for a set period, not indefinite.

Investment Objectives

Once you have identified your SMART goals, zeroing in on an investment objective needed to achieve the goals is next. Investment objectives are commonly expressed in performance terms, such as the return you (the investor) may need per year to achieve your goals. This is done in order to give you a better perspective on what return you are going to need in order to achieve your SMART goals. Your return objective will then dictate the ideal asset mix of your portfolio.

Investment Knowledge

Time and time again we hear, "Invest in what you know." Investment titans Warren Buffett and Peter Lynch propagated this belief. The more knowledgeable you are about a specific investment, the more confident and certain you will be regarding whether or not that investment is appropriate and suitable. All else being equal, greater investment knowledge means a higher risk profile and the flexibility to construct a portfolio with higher risk.

Current and Projected Financial Position

Your level of wealth plays a significant role in determining your asset allocation. In general, investors with higher levels of wealth tend to have greater risk capacity. Simply put, wealthy investors have more room for error in achieving their goals. Of course, this is not always the case, but as a rule it generally holds true. Conversely, investors with lower levels of wealth tend to have lower risk capacity, which can signal the need to construct a low-risk portfolio.

Time Horizon

The primary role that time horizon plays is to help you determine your balance between equity assets and fixed-income assets (see Figure 6-5). In the short term, equities are simply too volatile and possess too-high levels of uncertainty. On the other hand, fixed-income assets are significantly less volatile in the short term and possess much lower levels of uncertainty. As your investment time horizon increases, so too does the probability that equities generate positive returns and outperform fixed income. Over longer periods of time, equity returns become more stable, with more time for positive equity returns to offset negative equity returns. The returns of equities become significantly clearer and more predictable as your investment time horizon lengthens. The shorter your time horizon, the more emphasis you should place on fixed-income assets. Conversely, the longer your time horizon, the more you should overweight equities.

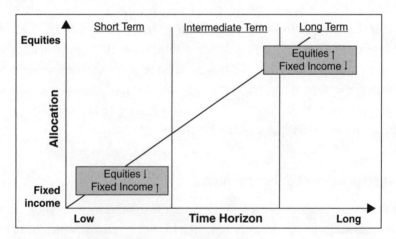

Figure 6-5 **Time Horizon and Portfolio Balance**

Income and Liquidity

Your need for current income and liquidity impacts how you allocate your portfolio. Investors who live partly off their portfolios will require highly liquid and higher-than-usual income-paying assets. Furthermore, investors in this position will typically have a much higher need for safeguarding the principal in their portfolios. As a result, overweighting fixed-income assets will be a top priority.

There are four primary categories of liquidity needs, which are presented in order of importance:

- **Emergency cash:** Having an emergency cash fund is by far the most important liquidity need you have. Conventional wisdom says that this fund should amount to anywhere between three to six months of your average monthly expenses.
- **Special needs:** Special needs are essentially those purchases or expenditures that are planned sometime within the next three to eight years. Examples include a second home or a grandchild's tuition.
- **Taxes:** There are two major taxes you will need to plan for: income taxes and estate taxes. Regardless of which tax is being incurred, Uncle Sam wants his money quickly, within 12 months for income taxes and within 9 months of death for estate taxes.
- **Savings and investments:** Savings and investments should not be mistaken for emergency cash. Each has its own purpose. Savings and investments allow you to take advantage of excess cash by forgoing current consumption and earning a return by putting it to work.

Tax Status and Tax Considerations

For investors with taxable accounts, attention should be given to the tax efficiency of investments. Investors with high federal tax rates will typically find it favorable to invest in tax-exempt municipal bonds rather than taxable corporate bonds. Tax management is very important since taxes on capital gains, interest, and dividends can reduce total portfolio performance, sometimes significantly. Deferring and minimizing taxes are strongly encouraged whenever possible.

The following are three areas related to taxes investors should consider when determining their asset mix:

- **Capital gains:** Capital gains taxes are those taxes on the appreciation of an investment that has been sold. Decisions to liquidate investments should be evaluated with respect to their specific tax implications. However, investment decisions take utmost priority over tax considerations. It is not prudent to hold an unsuitable investment just to defer capital gains taxes.
- **Growth versus income:** Taxes on interest and dividends received become taxable in the year received. But gains from the appreciation of an investment are not taxable until they are realized via a sale of the investment. This distinction gives investors some flexibility with determining when and where taxes are paid.
- **Tax-exempt investments:** Depending on your total combined tax rate, it may be ideal to substitute higher-yielding taxable investments, such as corporate bonds, with lower-yielding tax-exempt investments, such as municipal bonds. Why? The after-tax return might be higher with respect to lower-yielding tax-exempt investments than with higher-yielding taxable investments. It's the net return that counts.

Legal and Regulatory Considerations

Legal and regulatory considerations are much more prevalent with institutional investors than with individual investors. However, some of the legal and regulatory considerations you may encounter involve individual retirement account (IRA) contributions and withdrawals, employee stock option exercises, and challenges of restricted stock. Depending on the specific situation involved, you may need to build a portfolio with greater liquidity and cash positions.

Unique Preferences and Circumstances

Unique preferences and circumstances incorporate anything that cannot be categorized elsewhere and are typically unique to a particular investor. Examples of unique circumstances and preferences include the following items:

- Financially supporting a dependent parent or challenged adult child
- Excluding investments in energy or tobacco for socially conscious reasons
- Being restricted from certain investments due to one's job
- Filing for bankruptcy or having excessive debt payments

Investment-centric Factors

This section examines specific factors attributed to individual investments that in aggregate impact, along with investor-centric factors, the asset allocation decision and the resulting asset mix of investments.

Correlations

According to modern portfolio theory, an optimal portfolio is not just the sum of its parts. Rather, it is the sum of its synergies. Synergies are created by the interaction of the investments held within a portfolio. This interaction is commonly referred to as "correlation," and it is a critical input to the asset allocation process. Correlation is the technical term for measuring and describing how closely the prices of two investments move together over time (see Figure 6-6).

Positively correlated assets move in the same direction, both up and down. Conversely, negatively correlated assets move in opposite

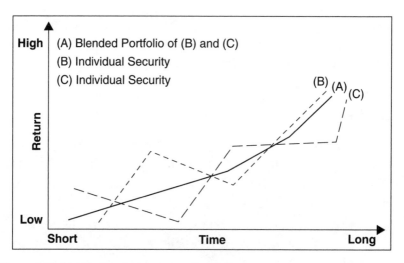

Figure 6-6 **Correlation Impact on a Portfolio**

directions. Correlations between two assets are expressed on a scale between −1.0 and +1.0. The more two assets are correlated, or move together, the closer they will be to +1.0. Similarly, the more two assets move in opposite directions, the closer they will be to −1.0. Two assets that move exactly together have a +1.0 correlation, and two assets that move exactly opposite to each other have a −1.0 correlation. Finally, correlations between −0.3 and +0.3 are considered noncorrelated. This means that the two assets move independently of each other. With noncorrelated assets, when one is rising in price, the other may be rising, falling, or maintaining its current price.

A properly allocated portfolio has a mix of investments that do not behave the same way. Therefore, you need to be concerned with the correlation variable. To maximize the portfolio benefits derived from correlations, you will need to incorporate investments with negative correlations, low positive correlations, or even assets that have noncorrelations. By investing in assets with low correlations, you are able to reduce total portfolio risk without materially impacting the expected return of your portfolio.

The greatest portfolio risk-reduction benefits occur during time periods when correlations across the board are low, noncorrelated, or negative. When correlations increase, risk-reduction benefits are diminished. Over time, some correlations will increase and some will decline.

Since you cannot predict which correlations will change or to what degree they will change over time, successful investors will allocate to a number of fundamentally different investments to reap the maximum benefits of correlation and its impact on the asset allocation decision.

Expected Total Returns

Building an optimal portfolio requires knowledge and application of both current and expected future returns. Without this knowledge and ability to model in expected returns, you might design a portfolio in which expected returns are not adequate to reach your SMART goals. Remember, you can't hit a target at which you are not aiming.

Risk Management Opportunities

It is important that investors have a grasp of how to manage and control risk when appropriate. This is important because the greater the opportunities to manage risk, the greater the potential to maximize return for the level of risk assumed. Investing in a basket or pool of similar investments minimizes investment-specific risk, or the risk associated with individual investments. Other opportunities for managing risk include the availability of derivatives, specifically put options, and the wherewithal to employ those derivatives. Put options don't mean much if you can't employ them to your benefit.

Inherent Volatility

Inherent volatility is the degree to which the price of an investment changes due to definable characteristics related to the investment. Greater inherent volatility translates into greater risk—and ultimately the need to reduce risk. Inherent volatility can arise from the following characteristics associated with a company's activities:

- Industry or sector
- Sensitivity to interest rates
- Sensitivity to changes in interest rates
- Float, or shares outstanding
- Degree of uncertainty in expected returns

Type of Returns

Are you looking for growth or income? How about deferred or immediate earnings? Each asset class can be classified as providing current income, market-value appreciation, or some combination of the two. In consequence, it is important to determine if certain investments match your needs or desire for current income. For instance, S&P 500 ETFs typically pay current income based on the dividends of the stocks in the S&P 500. Conversely, growth ETFs typically pay little to no dividends since growth stocks prefer to reinvest their earnings. For investors desiring current income, knowing the differences among asset classes—and the ETFs that track them—is important.

Trading Flexibility

You will soon discover—if you have not already—that some asset classes are much easier to trade than others. Depending on their inherent nature, some asset classes are less liquid than others, and that can mean higher trading costs in terms of one-half of the bid-ask spread. In addition, some asset classes are more difficult to invest in due to their availability, such as micro caps, small caps, emerging markets, and commodities.

General Nature

Aside from liquidity, trading costs, and availability, mentioned previously, asset classes also differ in regard to size, differentiation,

Investor Centric	Investment Centric
• Risk Profile	• Correlations
• SMART Goals	• Expected Total Returns
• Investment Objectives	• Risk Management Opportunities
• Investment Knowledge	• Inherent Volatility
• Current and Projected Financial Position	• Type of Returns
• Time Horizon	• Trading Flexibility
• Income and Liquidity	• General Nature
• Tax Status and Tax Considerations	
• Legal and Regulatory Considerations	
• Unique Preferences and Circumstances	

Figure 6-7 **Summary of Impact Factors**

definability, and completeness. Small differences between asset classes may not be material when your asset allocation is being determined; however, large differences and many small differences may create a scenario where the asset class is considered fundamentally different from others—a good thing for asset allocation purposes.

BUILDING AN ETF PORTFOLIO

The implementation of your ETF portfolio is rather straightforward since the vast majority of your premanagement decisions have been made during the design phase, with the exception of picking ETFs to build out your asset allocation. The process of implementing your ETF portfolio is much like the process of building a house or assembling a bookshelf: you simply need to read the instructions and follow the directions, so to speak. However, another important consideration in the step is deciding where to custody your portfolio. There are lots of alternatives. Will you custody your portfolio with a discount firm or perhaps a full-service firm? Discount firms make more sense if you know what you want to accomplish and do not rely on the insights of an investment professional. However, some investors may want the convenience of working with a dedicated investment professional. In this case, custodying your portfolio with a full-service advisor or independent broker is more appropriate. Once you build out your portfolio, you then move to the time-consuming step of managing your portfolio.

Picking ETFs

The process of picking ETFs can take a lot of time and requires research and comparisons among potential funds. Fortunately, by this point in the portfolio management process, you will know what general type of ETF to search for and evaluate in accordance with your already-established asset allocation. For instance, your asset allocation will most likely call for a large-cap U.S. exchange-traded fund, perhaps even a large-cap growth style and large-cap value style for enhanced allocation. Consequently, all you now need to do is to identify potential ETFs that fit that parameter and then compare them before ultimately selecting one or two. It's the comparison of similar ETFs that will take a little more time on your part.

MANAGING AN ETF PORTFOLIO

Managing your ETF portfolio is an ongoing process of monitoring and rebalancing your asset allocation over time. Changes in the values of your underlying ETFs and/or changes in your objectives give rise to the need for rebalancing. For example, if the equity market were to experience a significant rally over the next few months, then your portfolio would more than likely be overweight in equities. As a result, the risk and return trade-off profile of your portfolio would rise and possibly increase more than what is suitable for your situation. To return the portfolio back to your original plan—and before the market does so, thus giving back your gains—you will need to rebalance your portfolio holdings. Under this scenario, you would sell the overweight portion of your equity ETFs and buy the underweight ETFs—namely, fixed-income and possibly real asset (real estate and commodities) ETFs.

Monitoring Your ETF Portfolio

There are two areas where you should concentrate your time and energy to monitor your portfolio: performance monitoring and asset allocation monitoring.

Performance Monitoring

Evaluating the performance of your portfolio should be done on either a quarterly or an annual basis. Some investors might go crazy with the more volatile ups and downs of monthly performance monitoring. Long periods of time typically, but not always, smooth out performance. Unfortunately, evaluating portfolio performance is not as easy as it might initially appear. Why? First, there is the issue of evaluating a portfolio's short-term results when you have designed and implemented a long-term strategy. Only over longer periods of time can the benefits of your asset allocation and selected ETFs be properly measured. Comparisons made when short-term periods are used overemphasize security selection and market timing results at the expense of asset allocation policy. Second, there is difficulty in comparing a multi-asset-class portfolio to a benchmark. Which benchmark or benchmarks do you select? Simply selecting the S&P 500 for a multi-asset-class portfolio will not do the trick, as the S&P 500 is composed of equity securities only. The solution is to compare a well-allocated portfolio comprising equities, fixed income, and real assets against a blended benchmark that tracks the same markets.

Asset Allocation Monitoring

The initial asset allocation you have established should be compared periodically with the current asset allocation to ensure that there are no material gaps. Deviations above or below the band within which you allow each asset class to move are grounds for rebalancing, which is discussed next.

Rebalancing Your ETF Portfolio

Monitoring your portfolio is a constant process; this is in contrast to rebalancing, which is a task and therefore executed only at certain times. In consequence, knowing when and how to rebalance your

ETF portfolio is very important, as your ongoing portfolio performance depends on it. Essentially, there are two different methods, or triggers, you can use to determine when to rebalance:

- Valuation-based method
- Date-based method

Under the valuation-based method, after you have established a target allocation for a specific asset class during the portfolio design step, you then establish parameters (i.e., ranges) you will allow each asset allocation (as represented by an ETF) to move within before the need to rebalance is triggered. Thus, if you set the target allocation for large-cap value at 15 percent, you may let the allocation move plus or minus 3 percent of the total portfolio without triggering the need to rebalance. However, once the allocation moves outside the preestablished parameters, you will either sell or buy, depending on the overallocation or underallocation. Doing so will return the asset allocation to its target percentage.

The date-based method does not use parameters as does the valuation-based method. Under the date-based method, rebalancing is triggered on specific predetermined dates, typically either quarterly or annually. You let your allocations move in either direction and by any amount without rebalancing, and you make changes only on certain dates. For example, if you were using quarterly rebalancing, then you would buy or sell holdings irrespective of each deviation from its corresponding target allocation in order to return all allocations to the initial target allocations.

Note that both methods are used extensively by professional money managers; it's a matter of preference and design. You simply need to decide which one makes sense for your situation.

There are two primary costs you need to be aware of when rebalancing your portfolio: capital gains and trading costs (i.e., brokerage commissions and one half of bid-ask spreads). Depending on the cost basis, capital gains have the potential to significantly reduce your total return. Moreover, wide bid-ask spreads can cause trading headaches and higher costs as can high commissions charged by brokerage firms.

Regardless of the need to minimize rebalancing costs, always remember that investment decisions take priority over cost and tax-related decisions from a hierarchical perspective. It is not prudent to hold an unsuitable investment just to defer capital gains taxes. It's a conflict of interest that many active portfolio managers are confronted with frequently.

Advantages and Disadvantages of Rebalancing

The primary advantage of rebalancing is that your portfolio will continue to exhibit the desired risk and return trade-off profile given your objectives and constraints. As asset classes become overweight or underweight, as a percentage of the total portfolio, the risk and return trade-off profile of your portfolio changes. In order to return the risk and return trade-off profile to equilibrium, rebalancing needs to occur. This task can also be viewed as risk management. Another benefit of rebalancing is that you gain a better sense of how a portfolio operates and how best to manage it.

The primary disadvantage of rebalancing is the cost involved with doing so. Also, you need to take into consideration the amount of time required to carry it out.

Reallocating Your ETF Portfolio

Reallocating is the task of changing the target asset mix within your portfolio because of changes in either the investing marketplace or changes in your personal financial situation. For instance, if you have been collecting monthly income payments from your investment account and then realize you need to increase the amount to cover unexpected healthcare costs, then reallocating from equities to fixed income is in order. Furthermore, if new laws and regulations impact the tax treatment for certain bonds you hold, then reallocating from the existing bonds to more financially advantageous bonds should be considered. Irrespective of the event, reallocating your portfolio helps keep the asset allocation in line with current needs.

Tools and Strategies

This section details the tools and strategies that many sophisticated ETF investors use when managing their portfolios. These tools are presented to give you an introduction to what is available in the marketplace; they are not intended to be a detailed action-oriented plan for all investors to follow. Note that these tools and strategies are more aligned with active management and therefore tactical asset allocation instead of strategic asset allocation. Nonetheless, the choice is yours to make.

Tax-Advantaged Swaps

One of the key tax benefits of using exchange-traded funds is in the ability to swap them to reduce the tax liability of your portfolio. With ETFs, you literally can sell one with an unrealized capital loss to offset realized capital gains and then purchase a similar ETF with the proceeds all while retaining the asset allocation and enhancing the tax position of the portfolio. For instance, if your portfolio had $10,000 in realized capital gains and you had $8,000 in capital losses from a financial ETF, then you could sell the existing ETF—thus realizing the loss—and purchase a comparable (but not like-kind) financial ETF and therefore not alter the asset allocation mix of the portfolio. This strategy is not as easy as it may appear, but it is available to those investors who understand how the dynamics work.

Selling Short

Selling short is selling a security that is not owned by the investor with the anticipation of buying it back in the future at a lower price.

With selling short, an investor borrows shares of a security from a brokerage firm and turns around and sells those shares on the open market. The investor in turn receives the proceeds from the sale but then owes the shares back to the brokerage firm. As long as the price of the security declines, then the investor will profit. This follows the tried-and-true investing adage of buy low, sell high—or in this case, sell high, buy low. However, if the price rises after the initial sale, then the investor will lose money since he will have to replace the borrowed shares by purchasing the shares at a higher price. This translates into buying high and selling low—not exactly what investors should be striving for.

Leverage

Leverage is best described as borrowing money in order to buy more of an investment. For example, an investor expects that the return on a certain security will experience strong performance over the next year and will generate a return that exceeds the cost of borrowing funds. As a result, the investor purchases $200,000 worth of the security and borrows funds to buy an additional $50,000 of the same security. Thus, the investor will hold a security worth $250,000 by using only $200,000 of his own money.

When employing leverage, investors anticipate a higher return on the borrowed funds than on the cost of the borrowed funds. Investors borrow these funds from brokerage firms who charge them a rate of interest tied to a certain standard rate, typically the LIBOR (London Interbank Offered Rate). The use of leverage increases risk and therefore should be used judiciously. Leverage magnifies investment performance on both the upside and the downside. When an investment is performing well, leverage will generate excess returns. However, when an investment is declining in price, leverage will generate excess losses. When you combine significant leverage with extraordinary losses, a situation is created in which an investor can lose everything.

Hedging

There are different hedging strategies employed by sophisticated and institutional investors alike. For our purposes, the primary hedging strategy to use has the objective of reducing equity exposure to safeguard the portfolio against a potentially declining equity market. Consider a portfolio that is fully taxable with realized capital gains. Now envision that portfolio with high unrealized capital gains in all equity ETFs. If you desired to reduce your equity exposure to safeguard against falling equity prices, you can either sell your existing positions or hedge them. Selling them turns the unrealized capital gains into realized capital gains—and that means a tax liability. However, if you use hedging, you can reduce your net equity exposure without selling any holdings. To accomplish this goal, you can either purchase an inverse equity-linked ETF or sell short an equity ETF. Both methods allow you to reduce your net equity exposure without immediately producing a capital gains tax liability.

Specific Markets

Investors oftentimes will target specific markets, sectors, and asset classes. They will typically differentiate between geographic regions, such as European and Asian markets, and asset type, such as equities and fixed income. By targeting specific markets, investors can gain exposure to opportunities not emphasized in the overall market. For instance, if you wanted to gain broad exposure to global emerging markets, then you could purchase the Vanguard MSCI Emerging Markets ETF (symbol: VWO). However, if you were nervous about the growth prospects in all areas of the globe, except for Asia, then you could purchase the SPDR S&P Emerging Asia Pacific (symbol: GMF). Doing so would allow you to target specific markets, for better or worse.

Position Limits

To safeguard themselves from the loss in any one investment, investors can institute position limits that restrict the size of an investment to a certain percentage. For example, an investor institutes a 10 percent limit on how much any one position may make up part of her portfolio. Regardless of how well the asset is performing, no new investments can be made in the position above the 10 percent limit. This protects the investor from large losses, because even small swings in value can result in large losses when positions are bigger.

Buy/Sell Targets

In simplistic terms, a buy/sell target is the point at which an investor will either sell an asset because it is fairly valued or buy an asset because it is perceived to be undervalued. Investors will frequently place limit prices on securities, and when the investment hits one of those price targets, it triggers a buy or sell transaction.

Stop-Loss Restrictions

Regardless of an investment's perceived value, losses are still losses no matter where they come from. In consequence, stop-loss restrictions enable investors to cut loose (i.e., sell) losing investments once a certain investment reaches a predetermined level of losses. This predetermined point is the investor's maximum loss he or she is willing to incur on any one particular investment.

Order Discretion

Order discretion refers to how an order is executed with regard to time, price, and fill. Although each exchange and broker-dealer has its own unique sets of rules and offerings regarding order types, the following are the most common types of orders, which can be used together with other order types:

- **Market:** Stipulates that you want your order executed immediately at the current best price. Market orders are the most basic order types.

- **Limit:** Stipulates that the order is not to be executed until the price hits a certain level. Thus, an order to buy with a $40 limit when the ETF is trading at $41 will not be executed until the price drops by $1.
- **Stop:** Stipulates that the order does not go live until the current market price hits a certain price level. Once the order is live, then the order is executed as a market order.
- **Stop-limit:** Similar to the stop order but with one difference. Instead of the order becoming a market order once going live, it becomes a limit order.
- **Day only:** This order type stipulates that the order is good for only the current trading day. Most orders are assumed to be day orders unless stipulated otherwise.
- **Good 'til canceled (GTC):** Stipulates that the order will remain open until either executed or until canceled by the investor.
- **Market if touched (MIT):** Referred to as an "MIT order," this conditional order is executed as a market order if and when the security trades, or is offered, at a specified price or lower.
- **Market on close (MOC):** Stipulates that the order will execute at a price as close to the end of the trading session as possible. Also known as an "at-the-close order."

Options

An option is a financial instrument that gives the buyer the right to purchase or sell an underlying security (i.e., the ETF) at a predetermined price before a predetermined expiration date. Options can expire worthless, be exercised (thus taking ownership of an ETF with a call option and selling an ETF with a put option), or be sold outright to close out the long position. Sometimes selling your call or put option makes more financial sense than exercising it or taking the chance that the market reverses and the option ultimately expires worthless. For example, suppose you purchase an option for $5 when the price of the underlying ETF is $70. Two weeks later the price of the ETF rises to $75, and the option price rises to $10 as a result. Seeing the gain of $5 in your option, you sell, or close, the same option and receive the $10 premium from the option buyer. You will thus have locked in $5 (+$10 − $5). You are considered to have closed out your position without further action needed.

Call Options

Call options are used to take advantage of expected rising prices for a security. Call options give the buyer of the option the right, but not the obligation, to purchase the underlying security at a predetermined price before a predetermined date: the expiration date. If you are bullish on an ETF, then purchasing an option will allow you to profit if the price does rise before the option expiration date. If prices rise, then you exercise the option and purchase the security at below-market prices for a gain, or sell the option—thus closing your position—in the open market at a gain before the option expiration date. If the ETF price falls below the strike price and remains that way to expiration, then the option buyer is out the price paid for the call option, called the "premium."

Market Sentiment and the Purchase Decision

- **Buying a call option**: Bullish on the price of the underlying ETF
- **Selling a call option**: Bearish on the price of the underlying ETF

Put Options

Put options are used to protect investors from potential falling prices for a security. Put options give the buyer the right, but not the obligation, to sell the underlying security at a predetermined price before a predetermined date: the expiration date. Purchasing a put option will allow you to hedge your ETF position, if prices do fall before the option expiration date. If prices fall, then you exercise the option and sell your ETF at above-market prices. As with call options, you can also sell the put option in the open market at a gain before the option expiration date. If prices rise instead of fall, then the option buyer is out the premium or the price paid for the put option.

Market Sentiment and the Purchase Decision

- **Buying a put option:** Bearish on the price of the underlying ETF
- **Selling a put option:** Bullish on the price of the underlying ETF

Key Option Specifications

The following are five option specifications you should understand thoroughly before jumping into the world of ETF options:

- **Underlying:** The security (i.e., the ETF) attached to the option whereby the call option buyer purchases and the put option buyer sells. Generally there are 100 shares per option contract.
- **Contract month:** Denotes the month and year of the option contract expiration.
- **Expiration date:** Denotes the last day the buyer of the option has to exercise the option and either purchase or sell the underlying security.
- **Strike (exercise) price:** Denotes either the price the call buyer must pay to purchase the underlying security or the price the put buyer will receive to sell the underlying security.
- **Premium:** Denotes the amount of money one either pays to purchase the option or receives if one sells the option.

Maximum Option Gains and Losses

Call Buyer (long the option)

- **Maximum gain:** Unlimited (i.e., the price of the underlying ETF could skyrocket and keep going)
- **Maximum loss:** Premium paid

Call Seller (short the option)

- **Maximum gain:** Premium received
- **Maximum loss:** Unlimited (i.e., the price of the underlying ETF could skyrocket and keep going)

Put Buyer (long the option)

- **Maximum gain:** (Strike price × number of contracts × 100) − premium paid
- **Maximum loss:** Premium paid

Put Seller (short the option)

- **Maximum gain:** Premium received
- **Maximum loss:** (Strike price × number of contracts × 100) − premium received

CHAPTER 7

Practical Strategies for Picking ETFs

When you are evaluating common stocks, the typical criteria reviewed include such things as a stock's price-to-earnings (P/E) ratio, the price-to-sales (P/S) ratio, estimated five-year earnings-per-share (EPS) growth rate, and a P/E-to-growth (PEG) ratio, among many others. This analysis—as futile as I think it can be—is used by investors to determine whether a stock is overpriced or underpriced, all in the hope of guessing whether it will outperform or underperform the market. What about ETFs? Although ETFs have the same tradability as do stocks, always remember that they resemble mutual funds in many more ways than they do common stocks. As a result, using the same criteria to evaluate and compare two or more stocks in the same industry is not appropriate for picking ETFs. Rather, ETFs are a different animal, and you therefore need a different mousetrap altogether to capture the best in class ETFs.

In this chapter we will discuss how to evaluate, filter, and select ETFs to build out an investor's previously determined asset allocation. The paragraphs that follow should not be interpreted as being a tutorial on how to pick ETFs loosely and then buy them without any consideration given to the important allocation process and the quality of the overall portfolio. Picking ETFs first and working out an asset allocation plan afterward is the mirror opposite of what should be accomplished. You need to work on the overall design first and then work out the details. To use an example from everyday life, is it more appropriate to select new furniture first and then design a house around the furniture or design your house first and then select the style of furniture that fits each room? The design of the house—or, in our case, the portfolio—should come first.

In addition to conducting your own self-analysis on ETFs, you can also leverage the thinking of some of the top firms in the investment field. Three of the most prominent ETF-rating companies are Morningstar, Value Line, and Standard & Poor's. You may be able to get some ratings and information free of charge, but some of the commentary and higher-end research will come at a modest cost. This may or may not be of interest to you.

PRE-EVALUATION

Before you begin your evaluation and comparison of ETFs, you need to ask yourself a few questions to help keep you focused on the task at hand. These questions should be answered within the context of a previously established asset allocation. These questions include the following:

- Exactly what kind of ETF am I targeting?
- Will the ETF fill a need or gap?
- Is the ETF suitable for my personal situation?
- Am I familiar and comfortable with this type of ETF?
- What is the tax treatment for this type of ETF?

Chapter 11 provides a number of keys to ETF investing success. The aforementioned questions are discussed in greater detail in that chapter.

MOST IMPORTANT CRITERIA

In the paragraphs that follow we will discuss those criteria that are most important when evaluating, filtering, and selecting ETFs for your portfolio. These criteria include category and asset class, expense ratio, index tracked, volatility risk, historical returns, capital gains distributions, unique challenges, and legal structure.

Category and Asset Class

One of the very first criteria investors should investigate when evaluating ETFs is the category and asset class, including the potential subasset class, that best describes the ETF profile. From a broad perspective, ETFs can be equity, fixed-income, or real-asset linked. As you continue to drill down, you will find some ETFs that track large-cap growth stocks and some that track small-cap value stocks. Still yet, some ETFs will track corporate bonds, while others track real estate investment trusts. Because your goal is to build a comprehensive and optimally allocated portfolio, you will need a clear understanding of which category and asset class each ETF represents. To accomplish this task, simply have your previously designed asset allocation ready to go and then add ETFs where needed. Figure 7-1 provides a simplified template to help with this task.

Expense Ratio

Other than external expenses such as trading commissions, the most transparent cost you will pay when investing in an ETF is its expense ratio. An expense ratio is expressed in percentage terms, assessed on the market value of the ETF, and paid by shareholders on a pro rata basis daily. All else being equal, your top priority is to invest in an ETF or ETFs that have the lowest expense ratios. Obviously, if a certain ETF with a higher expense ratio offers something different and/or better, then paying a higher expense can be justified under practical situations. The difference in expense ratios between two

Asset Class	Allocation	ETF Option 1	ETF Option 2	ETF Option 3
U.S. Equities				
Large Cap	15%			
Mid Cap	10%			
Small Cap	10%			
International Equities				
Developed Markets	10%			
Emerging Markets	10%			
U.S. Fixed Income				
Short Term	5%			
Long Term	5%			
High Yield	5%			
Preferred	5%			
International Fixed Income				
Developed Markets	5%			
Emerging Markets	5%			
Real Assets				
Real Estate	5%			
Commodities	5%			
Money Markets				
Cash Reserve	5%	*Account Level*	*Account Level*	*Account Level*

Figure 7-1 **Simplified ETF Selection Template**

ETFs that track the same market index is commonly quite small and nearly immaterial. Finally, do not think that all ETFs are low cost. Leveraged, inverse, long/short, and some funds that track custom indexes typically charge much higher expense ratios than you might think for an ETF. Fortunately, this information is quite easy to find and therefore to include in your decision-making process.

Index Tracked

Aside from evaluating and comparing the asset class and total costs, comparing the indexed tracked is next in line for the most important criterion. Many of the most popular and largest ETFs track well-known market indexes such as the S&P 500 and the Russell 2000. Using this knowledge, you will be able to isolate ETFs that fit the asset allocation you have already identified for your portfolio. For example, if you are building a moderate balanced portfolio, then you surely will include both mid-cap and small-cap stocks. You might even divide both aforementioned asset classes to included both value and growth. Nonetheless, once you are armed with this goal, you can search for the ETFs that track the index. With the case of mid-cap and small-cap stocks the Vanguard Mid-Cap ETF (symbol: VO) and Vanguard Small-Cap ETF (symbol: VB) will typically suffice.

When evaluating an ETF, disregard the name of the ETF for the time being and focus on its merits. Why? Some ETFs are actually stealth ETFs, meaning the name does not convey the true objective of the holdings. For example, in light of the poor stock performance of banks and other financial companies in the last few years because of their risky, nontransparent investments, many of the so-called value-oriented ETFs could easily be renamed "financial ETFs" because of the much higher than normal exposure involved. You'll also find some "broad-based" commodity ETFs that should be called "energy ETFs" because of their overweight in the holdings.

Note that during this step you do not select the underlying indexer. Reviewing and selecting appropriate indexes is done when you are establishing your asset allocation.

Volatility Risk

According to modern portfolio theory—and pure common sense— investors should select the investment with the lower level of risk given a comparable level of return expectation. No one wants to assume any more risk than necessary, especially if the performance potential does not increase. When evaluating two or more similar ETFs, you should investigate and compare the two primary mea- surements of risk for each of the ETFs: beta and standard devia- tion, which are both discussed in Chapter 5. The higher the beta and standard deviation, the greater the volatility risk. Your job is to target the ETF with the lowest volatility risk without sacrific- ing return potential. Investors might want to seek the help of an online research company such as Morningstar, which provides a measurement of risk and communicates its risk ratings with common descriptive words such as *below average* and *above average*.

Historical Returns

Much like the aforementioned risk criterion, in this situation you want to compare the return potential of two or more similar ETFs against each other. To make the comparison, simply investigate historical returns with emphasis on 1-year, 3-year, 5-year, and 10-year performance, if that information is available. Given their youth, many ETFs do not have long-term track records, so you will need to use what you can find. Nonetheless, look at how well or how poorly the ETF has performed over each available time period; obviously, place greater importance on an ETF that appears for the period under review. Since most investors will be building an optimal portfolio comprising widely held ETFs, the difference between ETFs that track market indexes should be negligible. Comparing returns—although important—is typically not the difference maker some investors initially envision given their history and experience with mutual funds, specifically actively managed ones. Conversely, comparing returns for actively managed ETFs that track custom indexes or ETFs that track less common indexes can provide some degree of insight into the fund's management team, thus enabling investors to make more informed and better decisions on selecting the right ETFs.

As with risk, seek out a research company that provides information in easy-to-understand language; for example, Morningstar provides its take on the historical returns for ETFs and communicates its ratings in everyday language, such as *below average* and *above average*.

Capital Gains Distributions

Most ETFs do not distribute capital gains because of the creation and redemption process. Nonetheless, that does not mean that an ETF will not distribute capital gains because of any number of factors, including the most important: the structure of the ETF. As a result, when comparing two or more like ETFs, be aware of any capital gains that may have been distributed in the past and any that might be forthcoming. Investors who hold tax-exempt accounts or tax-deferred retirement accounts can place much less priority on this criterion than those with full-taxable accounts. With ETFs, the distribution of capital gains is quite infrequent and abnormal, but investing in an ETF without a history of capital gains distributions can help safeguard against the negative impact of taxes on capital gains even when an ETF has not been sold.

Unique Challenges

From time to time you might come across an ETF with what is best described as internal or structural challenges that are not apparent to the unwary investor. The two internal challenges of most concern are premiums and contango.

Although the creation and redemption process involving authorized participants is supposed to bring an ETF's market price in line with its net asset value, there are the very rare occasions in which an abnormal premium can exist. The occurrence of a premium is generally found in ETFs that track more obscure indexes, especially those found in the emerging markets, due to any number of financial and/or political reasons.

Contango, which is exclusive to ETFs linked to commodity futures, such as United States Natural Gas (symbol: UNG), is a pricing situation in which futures prices get progressively higher as monthly contract dates get progressively longer. As a result, when a monthly futures contract is rolled forward because of expiration of the existing contract, then the new contract must be purchased at a higher price than that of the previous monthly contract. Doing so creates negative spreads and decreases performance. It is for this reason that some leading investment experts strongly advise investors not buy ETFs where contango can become a problem.

In conclusion, when comparing two or more ETFs, investigate if any have experienced abnormal premiums or contango, and make your ETF selection appropriately.

Legal Structure

If you want to invest in a precious metals ETF, you have three different options available to you. First, you can purchase an ETF, such as the SPDR Gold Shares (symbol: GLD), that purchases physical gold and stores the bullion in vaults—primarily located in London. Your purchase gives you a proportionate ownership in the physical gold stored by the ETF. Second, you can purchase a precious metals ETF, such as the Market Vectors Gold Miners ETF (symbol: GDX), where the underlying holdings are stocks of publicly traded companies involved in mining gold. And finally, you can purchase an ETF, such as the PowerShares DB Gold (symbol: DGL), that gains exposure to gold through buying and selling gold futures contracts on a commodity exchange. Each of the aforementioned options comes with its own unique tax treatment—a $1,000 capital gain is not treated the same in all three funds. Chapter 10 provides a detailed discussion of the tax treatment nuances associated with different types of ETFs.

With the above example, you should be aware of each ETF's legal structure and whether or not it's a good fit for your portfolio. Unfortunately, there is no single "best" legal structure, nor is an ETF's legal structure easy to identify without drilling down below the surface. Nonetheless, be aware of this difference between various ETFs and take it into consideration when picking among comparable ETFs.

THE NEXT-MOST-IMPORTANT METRICS

In the paragraphs that follow we will discuss those metrics that are next most important when evaluating, filtering, and selecting ETFs for your portfolio. These metrics include tracking error, yield and dividend schedule, liquidity, legacy, and the number of holdings.

Tracking Error

Tracking error is a ratio expressed as a percentage that measures the unplanned deviation of return generated by an ETF compared to the return of an index benchmark over a fixed period of time. Tracking error is expressed as either a positive number for outperformance of the ETF or a negative number for underperformance. Deviations between the returns are generally very small and thus expressed in basis points rather than full percentage points. There are a number of reasons—such as the aforementioned expense ratio—why tracking error is higher for one ETF than it is for a comparable one. The top ETFs have the lowest degree of tracking error. Thus, when comparing an ETF against a comparable one, lean toward investing in the one with the lower or lowest degree of tracking error.

Yield and Dividend Schedule

For investors looking to receive a monthly or quarterly income check to help pay for typical living expenses, emphasize ETFs with attractive yields and frequent distributions. Identifying the dividend yield and comparing against a similar ETF is a simple, yet important, task. All else being equal, it's always advantageous to pick the ETF with the higher dividend yield, as oftentimes dividends can comprise a large part of total returns. In addition, when building an optimally allocated portfolio, look beyond the standard corporate or government bond ETFs and consider higher-yielding preferred or high-yield bond funds for part of your total fixed-income allocation. You might be surprised at the difference in yields, but you'll also need to feel comfortable with the potentially more volatile market price. Again, emphasize a mixture of different ETFs for a broad asset allocation.

Liquidity

Liquidity can be an issue with some ETFs, especially ETFs that track indexes that include less liquid and otherwise lesser-traded stocks, particularly those on the international front. Nonetheless, for investors looking to build optimal portfolios without reaching for high-risk and high-return potential, then the highly liquid and widely followed ETFs covering the primary asset classes and market segments are all that is needed. Investors should have no significant reason to look past the highly liquid ETFs and reach for something with questionable liquidity or other important metric.

The bid-ask spread is indicative of an ETF's liquidity. The smaller the spread between the bid price and the ask price, the greater an ETF's liquidity. Conversely, the wider the spread, the lesser an ETF's liquidity. As discussed in Chapter 2, liquidity for an ETF is a function of the aggregate liquidity of its underlying holdings rather than outright trading in the ETF itself.

When comparing two similar ETFs, take a look at the size of the spread between the bid and ask prices. The wider the spread, the greater the cost to both buyer and seller. All else being equal, select the ETF with the narrowest spread.

Legacy

We have all heard the expression, "Things get better with age." Although this statement is not entirely true in the investment field, there is some validity to it as well. Consider all ETFs that are launched every year, and fast-forward a few years. Some of the ETFs, even those considered good intentioned, will not make it past a few months to a couple years after inception. The 2008–2009 period saw numerous ETFs fail for lack of attracting enough assets under management to justify the operational expenses. Entire line-ups of ETFs were closed during these two years as they failed to gain traction with investors.

As an ETF investor, your job is to ensure that any ETF you invest in remains solvent and a going concern for years to come. Achieving this aim should not be very difficult, because the great majority of ETFs continue to exist in the marketplace after their initial launch. Nonetheless, when comparing ETFs, take a close look at the assets under management and how the assets have grown over the recent period. That knowledge can give you a clue as to how well or poorly the ETF is being received by the marketplace. Obviously, steer clear of those ETFs that seem stuck and don't appear as if they will get any better.

The best way to ensure that you are investing in an ETF that will be around for some time is to target only those ETFs with substantial assets under management or that have inception dates out many years. Once an ETF is over $100 million, it has gained critical mass, and you can rest assured that the fund will not be closed because of lack of investor interest. Furthermore, ETFs with inception dates past four years out should demonstrate a commitment from the ETF provider to keep the fund around for the foreseeable future, all else being equal. Assets under management and inception dates can easily be identified through the major news and research websites.

Number of Holdings

Although not a critical metric, the number of holdings by each ETF should be identified and taken into consideration. ETFs with a greater number of underlying stocks or bonds offer better diversification than ETFs with lesser numbers, all else being equal. Holding more underlying securities minimizes and diminishes the impact to the ETF from a negative event occurring to one stock or bond (or to a few of them). For example, if a bond ETF held 20 individual bonds and one of the bonds became nearly worthless when its issuer declared bankruptcy, then 5 percent of the fund would be impacted. However, if a different bond ETF holding the same bond in default held 100 bond positions, then the impact would amount to only 1 percent.

The type of legal structure and index tracked does play a role in how many securities an ETF might hold. Thus, comparing the holdings of a grantor trust, specifically a HOLDRs ETF, to a unit investment trust is not appropriate. That's like comparing apples to oranges. Furthermore, comparing a Brazilian ETF to a French one is not appropriate either. Make sure to limit your comparisons to similar ETFs for best results.

IMPORTANT METRICS

In the paragraphs that follow, we will discuss those metrics that are important but not as essential as the previously discussed metrics when evaluating, filtering, and selecting ETFs for your portfolio. These metrics include ETF provider, turnover, trading commissions, options availability, and early redemption fees.

ETF Provider

Although ETF providers strive very hard to make you believe their ETFs are different and somehow better than all the rest, from a pedigree perspective, the difference from one ETF provider to another ETF provider is not especially meaningful—particularly when you are evaluating ETFs that track market indexes and not subjective custom indexes. For example, when you are evaluating two ETFs that track the S&P 500, the name and reputation alone of the ETF provider should not make or break the decision about whether to invest in it, all else being equal. Nevertheless, some ETF providers have reputations for lower tracking error and some for an extensive lineup. These individual factors must be reviewed separately without including a bias for the ETF provider. Who the top ETF providers are will be apparent by evaluating the other metrics, such as expense ratio, tracking error, and yield. As long as the ETF provider has a reputation and history of offering sound investment solutions, then there is not a reasonable expectation that an ETF is better than a comparable ETF just because it was issued by a certain provider.

Turnover

One of the ways in which you can attempt to minimize receiving unwanted capital gains distributions from the ETF is to pick one with a low turnover. As you will read in Chapter 10, the distribution of capital gains by ETFs is very infrequent for most funds. Some bond ETFs and leveraged and inverse ETFs seem to be more prone to distributing capital gains, partly because of shareholder turnover. ETFs that track market indexes typically do not recognize capital gains and then pass through them to shareholders, which is something a comparable mutual fund might do. These types of ETFs track well-known indexes that are seldom reconstituted, an event that forces tracking ETFs to turn over their holdings. This means that if you stick with the top market index tracking ETFs, then you should avoid capital gains distributions. However, if you are interested in purchasing an ETF that tracks a custom index that is managed with active strategies, then comparing turnover is a good way to help minimize or avoid altogether receiving capital gains distributions. Most of the popular websites covering ETFs provide a measurement of each ETF's turnover, so your search and comparison should not be an arduous endeavor.

Trading Commissions

Depending on where you have your account held, your ETF trade executions can be somewhat low, if not entirely commission free. TD Ameritrade offers over 100 ETFs eligible for commission free trading, and Vanguard, Scottrade, Fidelity Investments, and Charles Schwab offer a number of ETFs commission free as well. Other firms will soon follow their lead. When you are deciding which large-cap ETF to buy out of a list of large-cap ETFs, saving some bucks with commission-free trading is a nice benefit. Of course, saving a few dollars should not make a difference in your investment suitability decision, but not having to pay for the initial investment and subsequent reinvestments and rebalancing trades can add up over time.

Options Availability

Some investors are very passionate about using options either for protection (i.e., insurance) or for generating incremental income from the writing of covered calls. If you are one of these investors, then selecting ETFs with robust options chains is ideal. Nearly all of the largest ETFs have robust options available, but a number of the smaller and newer ETFs do not. If you enjoy using ETFs to enhance your portfolio, investigating the options availability is a smart move and can be the factor that separates an ETF from its closest competitor.

Early Redemption Fees

Although the vast majority of ETFs do not impose any kind of redemption fee, some charge very minimal ones for early sales. When you read the fine print, you may find that some of the leveraged and inverse ETFs assess a very small redemption fee if they are liquidated within the first 30 days. Nonetheless, nearly all other ETFs do not have these kinds of fees. It is always good policy to confirm whether they do, especially since the industry is continuing to evolve and grow, and we never know what the future might hold.

CHAPTER 8

Professionally Managed ETF Portfolios

This book is intended to give you all of the tools and resources required to easily and successfully design, construct, monitor, and rebalance your portfolio using exchange-traded funds. But it is not intended to be a substitute for experienced professional management and counsel in each and every situation. With an endeavor as critical as managing your investments, it is not wise to take a do-it-yourself approach with every situation and not have professional help. Furthermore, many individual investors simply do not have the time, patience, or persistence to deal effectively with their investments over the long term. At the outset, many of them may have the motivation to put in the required time to fully address their investments, but they become less motivated as time goes by. In addition, individual investors may make some very common mistakes that an investment professional can help to overcome or avoid altogether:

- Making ad hoc fear-based revisions at the first sign of market weakness
- Fixating on each individual security rather than emphasizing the overall portfolio

- Failing to reevaluate their financial situation at least annually and then revising their plan accordingly
- Getting caught up in the hype of the market and losing proper focus and judgment
- Chasing the latest investment fads without concern for risk
- Blindly taking "hot tips" from questionable sources
- Not realizing that portfolio management is a process and not a quick and easy stand-alone decision
- Selecting investments purely based on historical performance

SOURCING, VETTING, AND WORKING WITH AN INVESTMENT PROFESSIONAL

Obtaining investment counsel is a significant step unto itself and should not be approached lightly. As with investors and their objectives and constraints, investment professionals also differ in their philosophies, processes, services, education, and experiences. Investment professionals work in many fields and hold varied titles, such as investment advisor, portfolio manager, financial planner, accountant, estate planner, insurance agent, and wealth manager. Over the last several years, most investment professionals have seen their roles expand, and now the lines among them have become greatly blurred. Nowadays it is commonplace to meet an insurance agent who is also a registered representative and certified public accountant who engages in the practice of estate planning.

With so many potential investment professionals to select from, the process can seem daunting. Remember, not all professionals are equal! Some of them may say the same things that others do, but when you investigate further you will discover significant differences. This section presents a plan, outlined in Figure 8-1, that outlines a number of criteria you should evaluate when vetting an investment professional to ensure a proper fit.

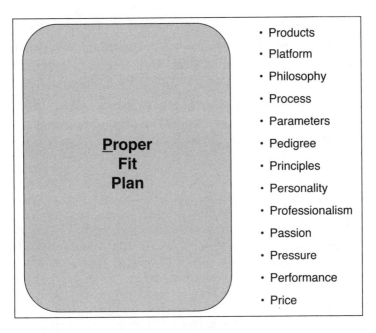

- Products
- Platform
- Philosophy
- Process
- Parameters
- Pedigree
- Principles
- Personality
- Professionalism
- Passion
- Pressure
- Performance
- Price

Proper
Fit
Plan

Figure 8-1 **Summary of the Proper Fit Plan**

Products

Before going any further with an investment professional, you'll need to ensure that he or she offers ETF investment management. You'll find that most investment professionals do offer this type of investment management, but some deal exclusively with either individual stocks (because they don't know any better) or mutual funds (because they make more money). Once you feel comfortable that an investment professional offers a solid ETF product, then and only then should you continue the vetting process. All major brokerage firms offer some type of ETF product.

Parameters

Just because an investment professional offers an ETF product, that does not mean it is what you are specifically looking for. Some ETF products are easily customizable to each client, but most are offered with model portfolios. As a result, the models offered may not provide the investment objective most appropriate for your particular situation. Perhaps the ETF product offers only ETF models based on asset allocation (e.g., low risk, moderate risk, high risk) and omit specialized models such as income generation and global allocation. Make sure to ascertain what types of ETF products are available and whether or not they are a good fit for you.

Platform

All major brokerage firms offer some type of ETF product principally employing internal platforms for creating and managing portfolios and executing needed trades. In contrast, independent advisors use platforms that oftentimes differ from not only those used at major brokerage firms, but also from other independent advisors as well. Some advisors use true managed platforms built and managed by third-party firms such as Morningstar, Genworth, and Brinker, while others create model ETF portfolios and custody accounts with discount brokerage firms and manage the models exclusively. Some of these platforms are turn-key while others are much more hands-on, depending on the needs of the client and expertise of the advisor.

Philosophy

When you are looking to get a better handle on how an investment professional manages ETFs, ask about his or her investment philosophy. Some investment professionals believe in a strategic approach, and others believe in providing a tactical asset allocation approach. Most investment professionals provide this information in their brochures. If they do not, then ask to see it. Furthermore, some investment professionals place significant emphasis on tax management, while others are less engaging. Specifically, ask about the degree of ETF turnover, how they incorporate tax management into their management process, and how they approach the issue of loss harvesting (i.e., selling investments with unrealized capital losses to offset previously realized capital gains) and ETF tax-swap strategies. Many investment professionals will strive to maximize the top line, or gross return, but the top investment professionals will focus on maximizing the bottom line (i.e., the net return). Remember, if you cannot walk away with it, did you really earn it in the first place?

Process

Investors should conduct investigations into the investment process employed by each investment professional under consideration. This includes such items as investment strategy revisions, use of derivatives and leverage, and buying and selling methodology. Some investment professionals employ top-down investment styles, while others use bottom-up styles. With ETF managed products, process is exceptionally important, since investment professionals do not have to concentrate on market timing and security selection. In fact, process is critical to the success of many types of companies, not just investment ones. For example, if you visit a McDonald's restaurant, you can often find that the entire staff is made up of high school–aged workers led by someone who's not too much older than them. It's the process that has enabled this type of business environment to become successful and has maintained that success through various business stages. The top firms are process-oriented.

Pedigree

Know with whom you are investing your money. This is perhaps one of the most important and commonsense lessons of working with an investment professional. Make sure the person who handles your investments and other key decision makers are qualified to manage your money. Investigate his or her education, professional designations (discussed later in this chapter), degree, and types of related work experience. Investigate how long the investment professional has been managing ETF portfolios and how much experience he or she has with overall traditional investments and portfolio management. Also inquire about how long the manager has been in his or her present role.

Principles

The question of personal principles of professional ethics and integrity is obviously not easy to answer when you first meet someone. However, nothing can cause your working relationship and ETF portfolio to suffer like the outcome of unethical behavior. Enron and Bernard Madoff are two examples of businesses that got involved in situations that went badly wrong from a clear lack of the professional principles of integrity and ethics.

The vast majority of investment professionals want to remain in the investment advisory business over their lifetime, and therefore they exercise highly ethical behavior. Building a successful investment management firm can take a significant amount of work, time, and money; however, only one lapse in professional principles can make it come crashing down. So you need to ask specific questions during the vetting process, review disclosure documents, and ideally conduct a background check as well. You can check with the industry agency that regulates the professional (e.g., the Financial Industry Regulatory Authority, or FINRA; the state of domicile; or the Securities and Exchange Commission) and any professional industry organization (e.g., Certified Financial Planner Board of Standards) with whom he or she might be associated.

Personality

Investors need to consider the personality fit before deciding to invest with an investment professional. Usually after the first meeting you will know if there is a personality fit or not. For instance, is the investment professional serious or humorous? What about you? Is she intense or low-key? Is the investment professional a golfer or boater? (People tell me you can't do both.) Is she dedicated to working out? And so on. Personality fit is not a high-priority criterion; however, not having a good relationship with your investment professional or not sharing things in common with her could complicate things over time.

Professionalism

When you entrust your savings and investments to someone, you expect—if not demand—that this person is professional and takes his or her responsibilities seriously. Some people like extremely professional and polished advisors; others like more laid-back and casual ones. The choice is yours. Irrespective of the level of professionalism you desire, working with an investment advisor who understands when to be professional and how best to serve your needs is of utmost importance.

Passion

Have you ever worked with someone who, although professionally capable, lacks passion for what he is doing and the job he has? We have all witnessed this phenomenon. In my judgment, passion is incredibly important, as it affords you a level of comfort with the fact that the person knows what he is doing and how to apply that knowledge to your portfolio. Passionate people are more caring and responsive to client needs. Furthermore, people passionate about their roles will proactively seek out ways to learn and absorb more knowledge about how to continually get better at what they do. In the immortal words of Vince Lombardi, "If you aren't fired with enthusiasm, you will be fired with enthusiasm."

Pressure

As with any professional industry, the investment field is fraught with salespeople looking to make a big sale—and corresponding commission—irrespective of whether or not the product, strategy, and price are appropriate for clients. Separating sales pressure from a strong appropriate recommendation is not always easy. Because some clients do not know what is best for them and for others that engage in bad investing practices, a stern and strong recommendation from an investment professional is warranted. Nonetheless, steer clear of investment professionals who put pressure on you to transfer your account to them and/or invest in a certain product or strategy. Instead, target the hard-working professionals who have the passion and desire to help people without engaging in sales pressure and who want to forge a long-term relationship with you.

Performance

Most investment professionals can provide you with some type of performance composite for your review. When reviewing the composite, be sure to identify which benchmark or benchmarks are employed (e.g., S&P 500 or a blend), the historical returns against the benchmark or benchmarks, the consistency of returns over long periods of time, the volatility of returns (especially in relation to the benchmark or benchmarks), and the statement of whether or not the performance composite conforms to CFA Institute standards. A statement claiming that the performance composite conforms to CFA Institute standards and is verified by an independent third-party firm is your best assurance that the performance results are accurate. Investment firms typically offer multiple ETF models, so focus on the relevant performance composites.

Price

There are multiple ways an investment professional can be compensated for his or her advice and services. The three most common with ETF investing are commissions, investment management fees, and hourly planning fees. Some investors will pay only one of these fees, but others will pay for two or all three. It depends on the fee structure designed by the investment professional. There is not any right or wrong fee structure. The best fee structure is what makes sense and is the best fit for you. As mentioned throughout this book, there are a number of discount brokerage firms that offer commission-free order execution on a list of select ETFs. Investment management fees are based on the total market value of your portfolio and are expressed in percentage terms. The typical fee is assessed quarterly and is approximately 1 percent for independent advisors and a little higher for full-service brokerage advisors. This structure is appealing because it motivates the investment professional to safeguard and grow your portfolio, thereby protecting and growing his or her fees at the same time. Essentially, one can say that this type of asset-sized fee structure aligns your interests with the financial interests of your investment professional. Lastly, hourly planning fees are charged by some investment professionals to compensate them for the work they do in planning and designing your portfolio. Most, but not all, investment professionals either do not charge this fee or waive this fee if they manage your portfolio. Nearly all advisors can provide investors with a written document outlining their fees and when and how they are payable.

CHARACTERISTICS OF TOP INVESTMENT PROFESSIONALS

To help you identify top investment professionals when you first meet them, this chapter presents multiple characteristics that define exactly what makes them head of the pack. Emphasizing these characteristics in your vetting process can help you find a suitable person and/or firm to select.

Substantial Expertise and Experience

Top investment professionals are typically highly educated and experienced, and they possess a strong grasp not only of the investing marketplace but also of how to combine their skill set in order to manage investments for long-term success. These professionals have a true passion and drive to manage money and help their clients achieve financial needs and goals.

Robust Operational Structure

Given that operations are the core of any investment firm, top investment professionals proactively create and refine their operational structures. Making up operational structure are such things as trading operations, broker-dealer effectiveness, pricing and valuation, and executive leadership. The top investment professionals strive to build, enhance, and protect their operational structure, thus enabling them to service the clients effectively without issue.

Defined Investment Strategy

For the most part, investment strategy is how investment professionals differentiate themselves from the competition. Doing so enables investment professionals to offer unique expertise, experience, and investment accessibility to investors. Investors with the greatest amount of clout and sophistication will seek out investment professionals who offer very specific types of managed money programs (e.g., ETF managed accounts). The top managers rarely deviate from established investment strategy, as they know where their competitive advantage lies. This also helps to brand an investment advisor.

Disciplined Investment Approach

Top investment professionals have clearly defined approaches to making investment decisions. Going outside their established guidelines is typically unacceptable and therefore rarely happens. For instance, investment professionals who have policies against the use of leverage beyond a certain point are generally highly disciplined to ensure that the threshold is not breached. Demonstrating consistency in a disciplined investment approach is very important to top investment professionals and a positive for institutions when investors are evaluating investment professionals with whom to invest.

Strong Risk Management

Risk management is one of the most common characteristics of top investment professionals. They recognize the need for sound systems and processes to identify when and where a model portfolio or investment strategy might be assuming greater risk than is acceptable. A strong risk management group at an investment firm will provide investors with comfort and confidence in the solutions offered by the firm. It also gives the necessary oversight into ensuring that the portfolios do not stray from established guidelines and thresholds for risk. Strong risk management groups will stop and restrain managers when they deviate from set policy and goals and potentially place portfolios at unacceptable levels of risk.

Responsive and Accessible Management

Top investment professionals recognize that they need to develop and cultivate an environment of open communication. Large institutions will demand it. Being responsive to investor issues relating to account management or client service is also a high priority. Top professionals know that it is much more difficult to gain new investors than it is to retain existing investors.

Highly Ethical

Top investment professionals want to remain in this business over the life of their careers, and they recognize that the default standard needs to be the exercise of professional excellence. They understand that even the slightest perception of less-than-professional integrity can have dramatic results on the firm—it doesn't take much to tarnish a reputation. These professionals are at the pinnacle of the industry and oftentimes the peak of their careers; therefore, they do not want to risk losing everything because of one lapse of ethical behavior.

MAKING SENSE OF "DESIGNATIONOLOGY"

The investment field has become an alphabet soup, so to speak, of professional designations. Most investment professionals obtain these designations for two primary reasons: to differentiate themselves from their peers and to gain the necessary education in order to benefit their clients and thus enhance their investment practices. When searching for professional help, you should place significant emphasis on investment professionals who have earned the right to use one or more of the following foremost designations. They are ranked in no particular order, and no one or two designations suggests that an investment professional is more qualified than another.

Certified Financial Planner

The Certified Financial Planner (CFP) designation is one of the most recognizable, most relevant, and most prestigious designations for an investment professional. Individuals with the CFP designation are well grounded in all aspects of financial planning, including investment planning, estate planning, income tax planning, insurance and risk management, retirement planning, and general financial planning. The CFP certificant, as he or she is called, must pass a number of module exams, including a final exam; accumulate three years of applicable work experience; and complete ongoing continuing education to qualify for the designation.

Certified Fund Specialist

The Certified Fund Specialist (CFS) designation provides a way for advisors to focus their business on mutual funds. Applicants must pass an exam on such topics as investment companies, performance measurement, and asset allocation. The Institute of Business & Finance, the sponsor of the CFS program, requires designation holders to complete ongoing continuing education credits.

Certified Public Accountant

The Certified Public Accountant (CPA) designation is also one of the most recognizable designations and one of the most difficult to get. In addition to earning accounting college credits, applicants are required to accumulate relevant work experience and pass a comprehensive exam. The focus of CPAs is geared toward tax preparation, although more and more CPAs are entering the financial and investment planning fields.

Personal Financial Specialist

Certified Public Accountants who wish to concentrate specifically on financial planning have the opportunity to obtain the Personal Financial Specialist (PFS) designation. This designation is awarded only to CPAs in good standing with the American Institute of Certified Public Accountants (AICPA). This designation covers topics such as estate planning, budgeting and saving, managing credit, and retirement planning.

Chartered Financial Analyst

Along with the CPA designation, the Certified Financial Analyst (CFA) may be the most difficult designation to earn. A CFA applicant must pass three rigorous examinations, accumulate three years of professional work experience in the investment field, and receive multiple letters of recommendation from professionals who are already members of the organization. The CFA is a common designation for investment counselors, portfolio managers, mutual fund managers, and investment analysts. All of the top practitioners in the investment management field either hold the designation or recognize its significant value.

Chartered Investment Counselor

CFA designation holders who wish to demonstrate their knowledge and extensive work experience have the option of earning the Chartered Investment Counselor (CIC) designation. CIC applicants must first obtain the CFA designation, be employed by a member firm of the Investment Counsel Association of America (ICAA), and must have accumulated at least five years of investment work experience.

Chartered Financial Consultant

The Chartered Financial Consultant (ChFC) is very similar in focus to the CFP; a Chartered Financial Consultant holder demonstrates broad knowledge of the financial planning field, such as estate planning, insurance, and investment planning. Similar to CFPs, applicants must accumulate a specific amount of work experience before earning this well-regarded designation.

Chartered Life Underwriter

The Chartered Life Underwriter (CLU) designation is targeted, but not exclusive, to insurance professionals. Contrary to its name, the CLU is not limited to only life insurance professionals, but nearly all CLU holders are involved somehow and somewhere in the insurance industry. Many other professionals not employed in the life insurance field have earned the right to use it. Applicants for the CLU designation must complete a 10-course curriculum.

Chartered Mutual Fund Counselor

Similar to the Certified Fund Specialist, Chartered Mutual Fund Counselor (CMFC) is a designation tailored to those who work primarily with mutual funds. To obtain this designation, CMFC applicants must complete a self-study program and pass a final examination on various topics important to mutual funds and professionals who opt to employ them in their product offerings.

Chartered Alternative Investment Analyst

The Chartered Alternative Investment Analyst (CAIA) is similar in nature to the Chartered Financial Analyst designation in content delivery and test taking. However, as the name implies, the CAIA emphasizes alternative assets such as hedge funds, private equity, commodities, real estate, and managed futures. If you are looking to invest in any of these alternative assets, then seek out a CAIA designation holder who has the requisite specialized knowledge and work experience.

Registered Investment Advisor

The term Registered Investment Advisor (RIA) technically describes an investment firm rather than a particular individual. A firm with this designation charges investment management fees based on the market value of the assets in your portfolio. To be designated an RIA, a firm must register with either the SEC or the firm's state of domicile. Individuals who work for an RIA are called "IARs," or "Investment Advisor Representatives."

INVESTMENT POLICY STATEMENT

Much like a blueprint for building a house, an investment policy statement (IPS), serves as a blueprint for building a structurally sound ETF portfolio. This document is important to the long-term achievement of your specific financial needs and goals when working with an investment professional. First and foremost, an investment policy statement helps you identify and learn more about your financial needs and priorities, how to best manage them, and the risks involved with achieving them. Secondly, this document allows you and your investment professional to gain a better understanding of your objectives and constraints and how to best manage your portfolio to accomplish your specific financial needs and goals. Without an investment policy statement, an investment professional may make inappropriate investment decisions such as incorporating high-risk investments in an otherwise moderate-risk portfolio or overweighting fixed-income securities in what should be an otherwise growth-oriented portfolio. Both situations result in a portfolio that does not reflect its suitable objective.

On the flip side, an investment policy statement alone will not guarantee success in safeguarding and growing your ETF portfolio. Rather, it will shelter your portfolio from ad hoc revisions made either by you or your investment professional to a sound, long-term plan.

An investment policy statement may take many forms, from including simple asset class targets to encompassing highly complex and oftentimes specific criteria. Some may even mention which investments an investment professional is prohibited from incorporating—for example, real estate, commodities, derivatives, foreign bonds, or those considered not to be socially conscious. An investment policy statement will assist you in maintaining a long-term approach when short-term market volatility may bring about stressful nights and misgivings about the plan.

Outline of an Investment Policy Statement

A properly drafted investment policy statement outlines the asset classes selected for investment and their respective target weights for your portfolio. In addition, many plans make mention of security selection and market timing strategies, depending on the investor and investment professional. A properly drafted investment policy statement clearly articulates your objectives and constraints as well as how to address and incorporate them within the portfolio management process. Your investment policy statement should make every effort to incorporate the following important items:

- Breakdown of your current portfolio
- Summary of your objectives and constraints
- Your optimal portfolio compared to your current portfolio
- The process for implementing your optimal portfolio
- The process for monitoring your portfolio
- The rebalancing process
- How the annual review process works
- Signed agreement between you and your investment professional

Benefits of an Investment Policy Statement

Articulating your specific financial needs, goals, and constraints provides a benchmark, or objective standard, with which to evaluate your investment professional. In addition, an investment policy statement also helps to curb unethical behavior on the part of your investment professional since your financial plan is clearly spelled out in written form for all interested parties to view. Miscommunications or actions such as playing the market or taking unnecessary risks are not only easier to discover but also much less likely to occur. Furthermore, an investment policy statement guards the portfolio against ad hoc decisions that impede your predetermined long-term investment strategy

Another significant benefit of using an investment policy statement is the resolution or plan when there is a change of investment professional. Due to various reasons, some investment professionals will manage a portfolio for only a short period of time before they move to another role in the firm or to another firm altogether. Since your time horizon may extend out many years, working with multiple investment professionals is not uncommon and a real possibility. As a result, an investment policy statement will ensure a smooth transition to a new investment professional.

Updating Your Investment Policy Statement

An investment policy statement should be reviewed and, if appropriate, modified annually. A comprehensive review of your return aspirations, risk profile, liquidity needs, time horizon, legal considerations, and unique circumstances should be made and any changes incorporated into the existing document. It is your responsibility to communicate to your investment professional any and all changes to your financial situation as soon as appropriate. Doing so will help your investment professional work diligently toward achieving your financial needs, goals, and objectives.

MANAGING YOUR MANAGER

Now that we have discussed the process of vetting investment professionals, we turn our attention to the importance and process of managing your manager through proper, ongoing due diligence. There are a number of reasons why this is important:

- Monitoring allows you to keep tabs on the your investment professional, the person most responsible for managing your portfolio and generating performance.
- Monitoring allows you to gain a better insight into how your portfolio is being managed, what is impacting the performance, and what value the investment professional is adding.
- Monitoring guards the portfolio against investment professionals making ad hoc decisions that will impede your long-term strategy.
- Monitoring allows you to quickly identify performance and ethical lapses and to make quick decisions to resolve these issues.
- Monitoring greatly decreases miscommunications and misunderstandings and allows for such occurrences to be quickly and easily resolved.
- Monitoring is a form of risk management and control.
- Monitoring helps keep the investment professional in tune with your needs.
- Monitoring assists the investment professional in understanding your objectives and guidelines.
- Monitoring ensures that your asset allocation does not stray from the optimal asset allocation established from the beginning.

Regardless of how you stay in contact with your investment professional—by telephone, e-mail, office visits, and/or social events—staying in contact is very important, as it ensures that all is well and plans are being followed. Keeping up on the latest happenings in the investment marketplace is another smart move.

Potential Areas of Concern

ETF managers, like managers of traditional investments, have certain areas that have historically shown greater areas of concern than others over time. In consequence, your due diligence monitoring warrants a review of the following areas that could impact the performance and success of your investment.

Change in Key People

When you work with an investment professional, you typically rely on one or two key people to make all of the decisions. These are the very people who have built the firm to where it is today and offer an alluring ETF managed product that initially attracted your attention and interest. If these key people leave, their talent and skill will leave with them. Filling the vacuum can be an unproven person or at least someone unproven with that particular firm. A change in key people commonly triggers investors to follow them or simply to seek out another investment professional altogether.

Prudence Issues

A good investment professional will be glorified at some time in his or her career. ETF management is a wonderful profession; however, it is also laden with opportunities for investment professionals to become overconfident and egotistical. This may cause them to believe they can deviate from the existing strategy and try something new and totally different. Rational and prudent investment professionals recognize this risk, and they safeguard portfolios from any such scenarios occurring.

Ignoring Stated Safeguards and Provisions

Safeguards are put in place to protect the investor and give the investment professional guidelines for how to manage the portfolio. When these safeguard provisions are ignored, that could present problems with keeping to the stated plan. Investors need to pay particular attention to how the investment professional is adhering to stated provisions, such as types of ETFs used, exposure to asset classes, number of positions included, frequency of trading, and the size of positions allowed.

Progress Benchmarking

Investors deserve to know if the investment professional is delivering on the stated representations made prior to the initial investment. Not only is this important to individual investors, but it is also meaningful to institutions that ultimately have a fiduciary responsibility to the individual investors who rely on their investment expertise.

Monitoring your ETF portfolio requires performance comparisons with appropriate benchmarks and related peers. Performance attribution is a key element to success with ETF investing. Many investment professionals evaluate the performance of a portfolio on a quarterly basis in order to appease the investor. However, evaluating performance is not as easy as it might initially appear. Why? First, there is the issue of evaluating a portfolio's short-term results when a long-term strategy has been designed and implemented. Second, there is difficulty in comparing a multi-asset-class portfolio to a benchmark. Which benchmark or benchmarks do you select? Simply selecting the S&P 500 for a multi-asset-class ETF portfolio will not suffice. The S&P 500 is composed of equity securities only. Thus, a portfolio comprising fixed-income securities and REITs simply would not be appropriate. The solution is to compare against a suitable blended benchmark.

Firing Your Investment Professional

As you progress with the monitoring of your investment professional, you may come to a point where a change in managers is warranted. This may be the result of lack of performance, comparably high fees, or simply a breakdown in the relationship. Nevertheless, making the change is not an especially easy task. Monitoring is a nonstop evaluation of whether or not to keep or fire an investment professional. In general, there is no set rule or provision as to how, where, or when to fire your manager. This process is rather subjective but must be approached with an objective mindset to collecting, understanding, and balancing the pros and cons.

AN ETF INVESTOR'S "BILL OF RIGHTS"

The following 15 "rights" highlight those provisions and limitations that serve to protect the natural rights of ETF investors. Consider this to be a quick and easy reference tool when vetting or working with an investment professional to help ensure the best possible outcome.

As an ETF Investor, You Have the Following Rights

▶ SECTION I:

To Suitable, Ethical, and Responsible Investment Management

▶ SECTION II:

To Courteous, Fair, and Professional Care and Service

▶ SECTION III:

To Honesty in Advertising, Marketing, and Sales Communications

▶ SECTION IV:

To Full Disclosure of All Risks and Potential Conflicts of Interest

▶ SECTION V:

To Thorough Explanation of Fees, Expenses, Penalties, and Obligations

▶ SECTION VI:

To Appropriate Background History on Each Investment Professional

▶ SECTION VII:

To Reasonable Time for Making Investing Decisions

▶ SECTION VIII:

To a Complete, Accurate, and Standardized Performance Composite

▶ SECTION IX:

To Timely Notices of Changes in Investment Strategy or Firm Dynamics

▶ SECTION X:

To Accurate, Complete, Understandable, and Timely Account Statements

▶ SECTION XI:

To Privacy, Confidentiality, and Safekeeping of All Nonpublic Personal Information

▶ SECTION XII:

To Verify Employment History and Investigate Disciplinary Records

▶ SECTION XIII:

To Quick and Just Resolution of Any Account, Service, or Relationship Issue

▶ SECTION XIV:

To Immediate Access to Invested Capital

▶ SECTION XV:

To Terminate the Engagement Quickly and Easily

CHAPTER 9

Simple Model ETF Portfolios

Now that we have covered the concepts and applications of ETFs, we turn our attention to what constitutes basic, but structurally sound, model portfolios using ETFs. For investors who are designing their own portfolios using ETFs, the task of establishing an optimal asset allocation and the ETFs to build out the asset allocation may seem time consuming and difficult. The aim of this chapter is to help alleviate concerns and provide helpful insights into ETF portfolio building.

This chapter is divided into two sections based on asset allocation models and specialized models. The asset allocation models are designed for investors whose objective is to build a portfolio that is low risk, moderate risk, or high risk. I've done away with the conventional "conservative," "moderate," and "aggressive" labels since I find them to be less descriptive of the portfolio and more descriptive of the investor. The second section of this chapter presents five specialized model ETF portfolios based on various investor behaviors and investment objectives.

ASSET ALLOCATION MODELS

The model ETF portfolios presented in this section (see Figures 9-1 to 9-3) are classified and titled according to their levels of portfolio risk—low risk, moderate risk, and high risk. The ETFs presented for each model portfolio are the same, with different weights to differentiate the level of risk.

Low Risk Model

Objective:	To generate a low risk, low volatility ETF portfolio that appeals to conservative and income-seeking investors.

Model Risk: Low	Model Net Cost: 0.23%

Model Holdings

ETF	Symbol	Category	Expense Ratio	Target Weight
Vanguard Long-Term Bond Index ETF	BLV	Long-Term Bond	0.11%	25%
Vanguard Short-Term Bond ETF	BSV	Short-Term Bond	0.11%	17.5%
Cash/Money Market	N/A	Cash	N/A	10%
SPDR Barclays Capital High Yield Bond	JNK	High-Yield Bond	0.41%	7.5%
iShares S&P U.S. Preferred Stock Index	PFF	Preferred Equity	0.48%	7.5%
Vanguard REIT Index ETF	VNQ	Real Estate	0.12%	5%
SPDR Barclays Capital Intl Treasury Bond	BWX	World Bond	0.52%	5%
PowerShares S&P 500 Low Volatility	SPLV	Large Value	0.25%	5%
ELEMENTS Rogers Intl Commodity ETN	RJI	Commodities	0.75%	5%
Vanguard Small-Cap ETF	VB	Small Blend	0.12%	2.5%
Vanguard MSCI Emerging Markets	VWO	Diversified Emerging Mkts	0.22%	2.5%
Vanguard Mid-Cap ETF	VO	Mid Blend	0.12%	2.5%
Vanguard FTSE All-World ex-U.S.	VEU	Foreign Large Blend	0.22%	2.5%
iShares JPMorgan USD Emg Mkts Bond	EMB	Emerging Markets Bond	0.60%	2.5%

Asset Allocation	Equity Size and Style	Economic Sectors

Asset Allocation
65%
10%
10%
15%
- Equities
- Fixed Income
- Real Assets
- Cash

Equity Size and Style

	Value	Blend	Growth	
	33%	22%	10%	Large
	22%	11%	3%	Mid
	0%	0%	0%	Small

Economic Sectors

Basic Materials	4.9%
Consumer Disc.	4.8%
Consumer Staples	22.4%
Energy	2.6%
Financials	10.1%
Healthcare	8.6%
Industrials	6.4%
Technology	3.7%
Telecommunications	3.6%
Utilities	33.0%

Figure 9-1 **Low-Risk Model**

Moderate Risk Model

Objective:	To generate a moderate risk, moderate return potential ETF portfolio that appeals to investors seeking balance in their portfolios.

Model Risk: Moderate	**Model Net Cost:** 0.24%

Model Holdings

ETF	Symbol	Category	Expense Ratio	Target Weight
iShares S&P 500 Index	IVV	Large Blend	0.09%	10%
Vanguard Mid-Cap ETF	VO	Mid Blend	0.12%	10%
Vanguard Small-Cap ETF	VB	Small Blend	0.12%	10%
Vanguard FTSE All-World ex-U.S.	VEU	Forign Large Blend	0.22%	10%
Vanguard MSCI Emerging Markets	VWO	Diversified Emmering Mkts	0.22%	10%
Vanguard Short-Term Bond ETF	BSV	Short-Tern Bond	0.11%	5%
Vanguard Long-Term Bond Index ETF	BLV	Long-Tern Bond	0.11%	10%
SPDR Barclays Capital High Yield Bond	JNK	High Yield Bond	0.40%	5%
iShares S&P U.S. Preferred Stock Index	PFF	Preferred Equlty	0.48%	5%
SPDR Barclays Capital Intl Treasury Bond	BWX	World Bond	0.50%	5%
iShares JPMorgan USD Emg Mkts Bond	EMB	Emerging Markets Bond	0.60%	5%
Vanguard REIT Index ETF	VNQ	Real Estate	0.12%	5%
ELEMENTS Rogers Intl Commodity ETN	RJI	Commodities	0.75%	5%
Cash/Money/Market	N/A	Cash	0.00%	5%

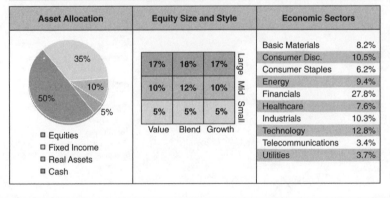

Asset Allocation	Equity Size and Style	Economic Sectors	
35% 10% 50% 5% ▣ Equities ▢ Fixed Income ▣ Real Assets ▣ Cash	Large: 17% 18% 17% Mid: 10% 12% 10% Small: 5% 5% 5% Value Blend Growth	Basic Materials	8.2%
		Consumer Disc.	10.5%
		Consumer Staples	6.2%
		Energy	9.4%
		Financials	27.8%
		Healthcare	7.6%
		Industrials	10.3%
		Technology	12.8%
		Telecommunications	3.4%
		Utilities	3.7%

Figure 9-2 **Moderate-Risk Model**

High Risk Model

Objective:	To generate a high risk, high return potential ETF portfolio that appeals to aggressive growth-seeking investors.

Model Risk: High	**Model Net Cost:** 0.20%

Model Holdings

ETF	Symbol	Category	Expense Ratio	Target Weight
iShares S&P 500 Index	IVV	Large Blend	0.09%	15%
Vanguard Mid-Cap ETF	VO	Mid Blend	0.12%	15%
Vanguard Small-Cap ETF	VB	Small Blend	0.12%	15%
Vanguard FTSE All-World ex-U.S.	VEU	Foreign Large Blend	0.22%	15%
Vanguard MSCI Emerging Markets	VWO	Diversified Emerging Mkts	0.22%	10%
Vanguard Short-Term Bond ETF	BSV	Short-Term Bond	0.11%	0%
Vanguard Long-Term Bond Index ETF	BLV	Long-Term Bond	0.11%	0%
SPDR Barclays Capital High Yield Bond	JNK	High-Yield Bond	0.40%	5%
iShares S&P U.S. Preferred Stock Index	PFF	Preferred Equity	0.48%	0%
SPDR Barclays Capital Intl Treasury Bond	BWX	World Bond	0.50%	0%
iShares JPMorgan USD Emg Mkts Bond	EMB	Emerging Markets Bond	0.60%	5%
Vanguard REIT Index ETF	VNQ	Real Estate	0.12%	8%
ELEMENTS Rogers Intl Commodity ETN	RJI	Commodities	0.75%	8%
Cash/Money Market	N/A	Cash	0.00%	5%

Asset Allocation	Equity Size and Style	Economic Sectors

Asset Allocation	Equity Size and Style			Economic Sectors	
10% 70% 15% 5% □Equities □Fixed Income □Real Assets ■Cash				Basic Materials	7.8%
				Consumer Disc.	10.8%
	16% **17%** **17%** (Large)			Consumer Staples	6.3%
	11% **12%** **11%** (Mid)			Energy	9.2%
				Financials	27.5%
	6% **6%** **5%** (Small)			Healthcare	8.0%
	Value Blend Growth			Industrials	10.6%
				Technology	13.0%
				Telecommunications	3.2%
				Utilities	3.8%

Figure 9-3 **High-Risk Model**

SPECIALIZED ALLOCATION MODELS

The model ETF portfolios presented in this section (see Figures 9-4 to 9-8) are based on the behavior and investment objective a particular investor might have. For the most part, the asset allocation models should be sufficient for investors, but sometimes a more focused ETF portfolio may be designed. Although the percentage weightings for each model are the same, each model employs different ETFs based on its objective.

Bullish Model

Objective:	An aggressive strategy to take advantage of anticipated strong returns in the equity and real asset markets.

Model Risk: Very High	Model Net Cost: 0.38%

Model Holdings

ETF	Symbol	Category	Expense Ratio	Target Weight
Russell 2000 High Beta	SHBT	Technology	0.63%	12%
PowerShares S&P Emerging Markets High Beta	EEHB	Emerging Markets	0.60%	12%
PowerShares QQQ	QQQ	Large Growth	0.20%	12%
Vanguard Energy	VDE	Equity Energy	0.19%	10%
PowerShares DB Base Metals	DBB	Commodities Industrial Metals	0.76%	10%
Vanguard REIT Index	VNQ	Real Estate	0.12%	8%
PowerShares S&P 500 High Beta	SPHB	Mid-Cap Value	0.25%	8%
Vanguard Mid Cap	VO	Mid-Cap Blend	0.12%	8%
Vanguard FTSE All-World Ex-US	VEU	Foreign Large Blend	0.22%	5%
SPDR S&P Emerging Asia Pacific	GMF	Pacific/Asia ex-Japan Equity	0.60%	5%
SPDR Barclays Capital High Yield Bond	JNK	High-Yield Bond	0.41%	5%
Vanguard Consumer Discretionary	VDC	Consumer Discretionary	0.19%	5%

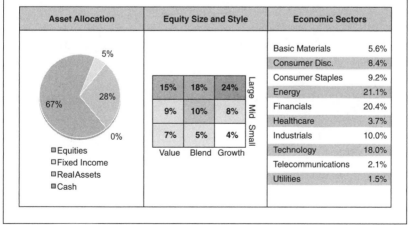

Asset Allocation	Equity Size and Style	Economic Sectors	
Equities 67%		Basic Materials	5.6%
Fixed Income 0%	Large: Value 15%, Blend 18%, Growth 24%	Consumer Disc.	8.4%
Real Assets 28%	Mid: Value 9%, Blend 10%, Growth 8%	Consumer Staples	9.2%
Cash 5%	Small: Value 7%, Blend 5%, Growth 4%	Energy	21.1%
		Financials	20.4%
		Healthcare	3.7%
		Industrials	10.0%
		Technology	18.0%
		Telecommunications	2.1%
		Utilities	1.5%

Figure 9-4 **Bullish Model**

Defensive Model

Objective:	A contrarian strategy to protect and/or profit from an anticipated weak equity market.

Model Risk: Moderate	Model Net Cost: 0.45%

Model Holdings

ETF	Symbol	Category	Expense Ratio	Target Weight
SPDR Gold Shares	GLD	Precious Metals	0.40%	12%
ELEMENTS S&P Commodity Trends	LSC	Managed Futures	0.75%	12%
Vanguard Extended Duration Treasury	EDV	Long Government	0.13%	12%
PowerShares S&P 500 BuyWrite	PBP	Long/Short Equity	0.75%	10%
WisdomTree Managed Futures	WDTI	Managed Futures	0.95%	10%
Vanguard Consumer Staples	VDC	Consumer Staples	0.19%	8%
Vanguard Utilities	VPU	Utilities	0.19%	8%
iShares Barclays TIPS Bond	TIP	Inflation-Protected Bond	0.20%	8%
JPMorgan Alerian MLP Index	AMJ	Equity Energy	0.85%	5%
PIMCO Enhanced Short Maturity Strgy	MINT	Short-Term Bond	0.35%	5%
PowerShares S&P 500 Low Volatility	SPLV	Large Value	0.25%	5%
iShares Barclays 3-7 Year Treasury Bond	IEI	Intermediate Governmen	0.15%	5%

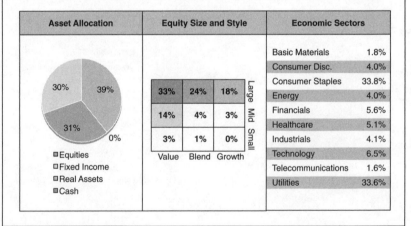

Asset Allocation	Equity Size and Style	Economic Sectors

Asset Allocation	Equity Size and Style	Economic Sectors	
30% / 39% / 31% / 0%	Large: 33% 24% 18% / Mid: 14% 4% 3% / Small: 3% 1% 0% (Value Blend Growth)	Basic Materials	1.8%
Equities		Consumer Disc.	4.0%
Fixed Income		Consumer Staples	33.8%
Real Assets		Energy	4.0%
Cash		Financials	5.6%
		Healthcare	5.1%
		Industrials	4.1%
		Technology	6.5%
		Telecommunications	1.6%
		Utilities	33.6%

Figure 9-5 **Defensive Model**

Sideways Model

Objective:	To generate high total returns through appreciation, but more importantly through consistent dividends and interest.

Model Risk: Moderate	**Model Net Cost:** 0.60%

Model Holdings

ETF	Symbol	Category	Expense Ratio	Target Weight
JPMorgan Alerian MLP Index	AMJ	Equity Energy	0.85%	12%
iShares S&P U.S. Preferred Stock Index	PFF	Preferred Equity	0.48%	12%
ELEMENTS S&P Commodity Trends	LSC	Managed Futures	0.75%	12%
SPDR Barclays Capital High Yield Bond	JNK	High-Yield Bond	0.40%	10%
PowerShares S&P 500 BuyWrite	PBP	Long/Short Equity	0.75%	10%
SPDR S&P Dividend	SDY	Large Value	0.36%	8%
SPDR Barclays Capital Convertible Securities	CWB	Convertibles	0.41%	8%
PowerShares Senior Loan Portfolio	BKLN	Bank Loan	0.83%	8%
WisdomTree Intl. Dividend ex-Financials	DOO	Foreign Large Value	0.58%	5%
Vanguard REIT	VNQ	REIT	0.12%	5%
PowerShares DB G10 Currency Harvest	DBV	Currency	0.81%	5%
PowerShares Financial Preferred	PGF	Preferred Equity	0.66%	5%

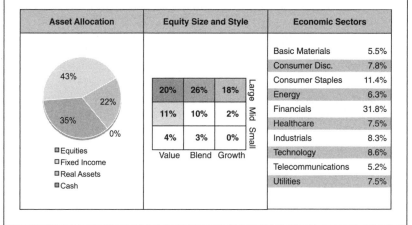

Asset Allocation	Equity Size and Style	Economic Sectors	
43% (Equities) 35% 22% 0% ▫Equities ▫Fixed Income ▫Real Assets ▫Cash	Value Blend Growth / Large Mid Small: 20% 26% 18% / 11% 10% 2% / 4% 3% 0%	Basic Materials	5.5%
		Consumer Disc.	7.8%
		Consumer Staples	11.4%
		Energy	6.3%
		Financials	31.8%
		Healthcare	7.5%
		Industrials	8.3%
		Technology	8.6%
		Telecommunications	5.2%
		Utilities	7.5%

Figure 9-6 **Sideways Model**

Global Allocation Model

Objective:	To allocate across the entire global marketplace with a balanced asset allocation.

Model Risk: Moderately High	Model Net Cost: 0.39%

Model Holdings

ETF	Symbol	Category	Expense Ratio	Target Weight
SPDR Barclays Capital Intl Treasury Bond	BWX	World Bond	0.52%	12%
Vanguard Total World Stock Index	VT	World Stock	0.25%	12%
Vanguard FTSE All-World ex-US	VEU	Foreign Large Blend	0.22%	12%
PowerShares Intl Corporate Bond	PICB	World Bond	0.50%	10%
Vanguard MSCI Emerging Markets	VWO	Diversified Emerging Mkts	0.22%	10%
SPDR DB Intl Govt Infl-Protected Bond	WIP	World Bond	0.52%	8%
SPDR Dow Jones Global Real Estate	RWO	Global Real Estate	0.50%	8%
ELEMENTS Rogers Intl Commodity	RJI	Commodities Broad Basket	0.75%	8%
SPDR S&P International Dividend	DWX	Foreign Large Value	0.46%	5%
Vanguard Short-Term Bond	BSV	Short-Term Bond	0.11%	5%
Vanguard MSCI Pacific	VPL	Diversified Pacific/Asia	0.14%	5%
iShares S&P Global Materials	MXI	Natural Resources	0.48%	5%

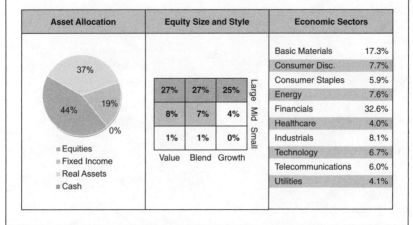

Asset Allocation	Equity Size and Style	Economic Sectors	
37%		Basic Materials	17.3%
19%	27% 27% 25% (Large)	Consumer Disc.	7.7%
44%	8% 7% 4% (Mid)	Consumer Staples	5.9%
0%	1% 1% 0% (Small)	Energy	7.6%
■ Equities	Value Blend Growth	Financials	32.6%
■ Fixed Income		Healthcare	4.0%
■ Real Assets		Industrials	8.1%
■ Cash		Technology	6.7%
		Telecommunications	6.0%
		Utilities	4.1%

Figure 9-7 **Global Allocation Model**

Income Focused Model

Objective:	To generate income from both equity dividends and bond interest from U.S. and international assets.

Model Risk: Low	Model Net Cost: 0.39%

Model Holdings

ETF	Symbol	Category	Expense Ratio	Target Weight
JPMorgan Alerian MLP Index	AMJ	Equity Energy	0.85%	12%
iShares S&P U.S. Preferred Stock Index	PFF	Preferred Equity	0.48%	12%
Vanguard Long-Term Bond	BLV	Long-Term Bond	0.11%	12%
SPDR Barclays Capital High Yield Bond	JNK	High-Yield Bond	0.40%	10%
Utilities Select Sector SPDR	XLU	Utilities	0.19%	10%
SPDR S&P Dividend	SDY	Large Value	0.36%	8%
WisdomTree Intl. Dividend ex-Financials	DOO	Foreign Large Value	0.58%	8%
Vanguard Intermediate-Term Bond	BIV	Intermediate-Term Bond	0.11%	8%
PowerShares Senior Loan Portfolio	BKLN	Bank Loan	0.83%	5%
Vanguard REIT	VNQ	REIT	0.12%	5%
PowerShares International Corporate Bond	PICB	World Bond	0.50%	5%
Vanguard Short-Term Bond	BSV	Short-Term Bond	0.11%	5%

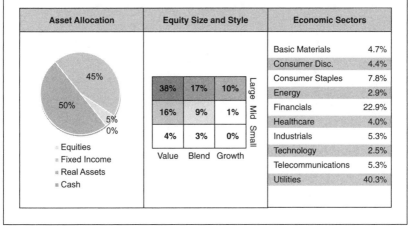

Asset Allocation	Equity Size and Style	Economic Sectors

Asset Allocation
45%
50%
5%
0%
- Equities
- Fixed Income
- Real Assets
- Cash

Equity Size and Style

	Value	Blend	Growth	
Large	38%	17%	10%	
Mid	16%	9%	1%	
Small	4%	3%	0%	

Economic Sectors

Basic Materials	4.7%
Consumer Disc.	4.4%
Consumer Staples	7.8%
Energy	2.9%
Financials	22.9%
Healthcare	4.0%
Industrials	5.3%
Technology	2.5%
Telecommunications	5.3%
Utilities	40.3%

Figure 9-8 **Income-Focused Model**

CHAPTER 10

ETF Tax Treatment Nuances

One of the primary advantages of ETFs over mutual funds is the high tax efficiency they provide. However, that does not mean that ETFs do not have tax consequences and that all tax consequences are simple, easy, and straightforward—on the contrary. Depending on the legal structure involved and the type of income distributed, the tax treatment for ETFs can vary greatly; it's not as cut-and-dried as you might think. In addition, depending on what type of investment account you have (e.g., fully taxable, tax-deferred retirement account, or tax-exempt investor), you might not have to give much consideration to ETF tax treatment at all. But for investors with taxable accounts, this chapter is a must-read.

The paragraphs that follow will discuss some of the most important differences—or tax nuances—by type of ETF and type of income received. This information does not replace advice from your tax advisor who should be consulted in such important matters. Refer to Figure 10-1—a tax chart—as we discuss both ordinary income and capital gains throughout this chapter.

| 2008 – 2012 | | | 2013 – | | |
| If... | Then... | | If... | Then... | |
Ordinary Income Tax Rate	Short-Term Capital Gains	Long-Term Capital Gains	Ordinary Income Tax Rate	Short-Term Capital Gains	Long-Term Capital Gains
10%	10%	0%	15%	15%	10%
15%	15%	0%	15%	15%	10%
25%	25%	15%	28%	28%	20%
28%	28%	15%	31%	31%	20%
33%	33%	15%	36%	36%	20%
35%	35%	15%	39.6%	39.6%	20%

Figure 10-1 **Tax Treatment for Ordinary Income and Capital Gains**

CAPITAL GAINS

This section discusses three ways, from the most common to the least common, you as an ETF investor might be subject to capital gains tax liabilities. These ways consist of selling shares of your ETF holding, receiving capital gains in cash that were generated and distributed by the ETF, and taking receipt of a premium when writing covered calls on ETFs.

Selling Shares of an ETF

When you sell shares of an ETF or another capital asset such as stock or a mutual fund, you are highly likely to generate either capital gains or capital losses. When the selling price is below what you paid (i.e., your cost basis) for the ETF, then you will recognize a capital loss. Conversely, when you sell shares of your ETF at a price above your cost basis, then you will recognize a capital gain. Furthermore, if you held the ETF for one year or less, then your capital gain is considered to be a short-term capital gain. ETF shares held for longer than one year and then sold qualify for the more tax-advantageous long-term capital gains rate. The recognition of both short- and long-term losses works the same way.

According to the present tax code (the Internal Revenue Code, or IRC), which is set to expire at the end of 2012, long-term capital gains are taxed at 15 percent for higher-income brackets, and there is no taxation for lower-income brackets. At the same time, short-term capital gains are taxed at the investor's ordinary tax rate, which is higher than a long-term capital gains tax rate. Capital losses are not taxed; instead, they are used to offset capital gains and sometimes ordinary income, to a limit.

Fund-Level Distributions

Although ETFs are highly tax efficient, they can and do distribute capital gains to their shareholders somewhat like mutual funds do but with much smaller dollar amounts. The distribution of capital gains is quite limited but can happen to even the biggest and most well-known ETFs and ETF providers. For 2011, out of its 200+ ETFs, iShares reported capital gains distributions for only two ETFs. Reporting absolutely zero capital gains distributions for their entire ETF lineup includes First Trust with over 60 ETFs in the marketplace, ProShares with over 125 ETFs, Russell with 24 ETFs, Rydex with 37 ETFs, and a handful of other providers. On the flip side, Direxion held the top spot for the largest dollar amount of capital gains distributed by one ETF. Of the top ten ETFs with the largest total capital gains distributions for 2011 (see Figure 10-2), three were

No.	ETF	Symbol	Provider	Total Gains	Short-Term	Long-Term
1	Daily Latin America Bull 3x Shares	LBJ	Direxion	$6.12	$0.66	$5.45
2	WisdomTree Dreyfus Brazilian Real	BZF	WisdomTree	$5.73	$2.32	$3.40
3	WisdomTree Dreyfus Commodity Currency	CCX	WisdomTree	$5.06	$2.20	$2.86
4	Market Vectors Brazil Small-Cap	BRF	Van Eck	$4.01	$0.20	$3.82
5	Columbia Growth Equity Strategy	RPX	Columbia	$3.94	$1.32	$2.61
6	Columbia Concentrated Large Cap Value	GVT	Columbia	$3.41	$2.20	$1.21
7	WisdomTree Dreyfus Indian Rupee	ICN	WisdomTree	$3.28	$3.28	-
8	Enhanced Core Bond	GIY	Guggenheim	$2.91	$1.36	$1.55
9	Daily Retail Bull 3x	RETL	Direxion	$2.90	$1.49	$1.41
10	Columbia Large-Cap Growth Equity	RWG	Columbia	$2.61	$1.15	$1.46

Figure 10-2 **Top 10 ETFs with the Largest Total Capital Gains Distributions for 2011**

managed by Columbia and three from WisdomTree. If you were to expand the list to observe the top twenty, then you would see Direxion with the most listed ETFs for capital gains distributions in 2011.

Writing Covered Calls

Under the current Internal Revenue Code, both ETFs and options are considered to be capital assets; thus, any gain from these investments is taxed as a capital gain rather than as ordinary income. Furthermore, with the exception of options known as LEAPS (Long-Term Equity AnticiPation Securities), options have maximum maturities of nine months, which means option premiums received are usually considered short-term capital gains. However, the mere collection of the option premium does not trigger a taxable event like the selling of an ETF. The option premium is held in suspense until one of three events occur. First, if the call option expires worthless, then the entire call option premium received is considered a short-term capital gain. Second, if the call option is exercised by the option buyer and the ETF shares are assigned, then the option transaction becomes part of the ETF transaction. That means that the premium received would be added to the strike price received, less all trading costs. Third, if the call option is purchased back, thus closing out the option, then the difference between the premium amount received and premium amount paid is considered a capital gain (or loss). Finally, if you are the writer of a call or put option and you put the option back before it expires, then your gain (or loss) reported is considered short-term no matter how long you held the option.

DIVIDEND AND INTEREST INCOME

This section discusses numerous tax twists associated with dividend and interest income that you, the ETF investor, might be subject to, depending on the type of ETF held in your portfolio

U.S. Equity (Common) Stock ETFs

Although not all equity ETFs pay dividends to shareholders, those that do typically distribute them on a quarterly basis. Under the current tax relief legislation—which is set to expire at the end of 2012 but may be extended—equity dividends are classified in one of two ways: ordinary and qualified. (Anyone who prepares his or her own taxes is probably very familiar with these terms.) If your dividend is classified as ordinary, then the tax rate is the same as your income tax rate. However, if certain criteria are met, then your dividend is considered to be qualified and thus receives more advantageous tax treatment. According to the IRS, qualified dividends are taxed at the lower long-term capital gains tax rate rather than at the higher tax rate for an individual's ordinary income. Currently, for those in the 10 percent and 15 percent ordinary income tax brackets, the tax rate for qualified dividends is 0 percent. For those in the 25 percent and higher brackets, the tax rate is 15 percent—the same rate as for capital gains.

In order to be considered qualified, the dividend must meet all of the following criteria:

- The dividend must be paid between January 1, 2003, and December 31, 2012.
- It must be paid by a U.S. corporation, by a corporation incorporated in a U.S. possession, by a foreign corporation located in a country that is eligible for benefits under a U.S. tax treaty that meets certain criteria, or on a foreign corporation's stock that can be readily traded on an established U.S. stock market such as an American depositary receipt (ADR).
- The dividend must satisfy holding period requirements: An investor must have held the stock for more than 60 days during the 121-day period that begins 60 days before the ex-dividend date. (The ex-dividend date is the first date following the declaration of a dividend on which the

buyer of a stock is not entitled to receive the next dividend payment.) When counting the number of days you held the stock, include the day you disposed of the stock but not the day you acquired it.

Any dividends that fail to satisfy the aforementioned criteria are considered to be ordinary dividends and thus subject to the higher tax rates. Real estate investment trusts—and therefore REIT ETFs—typically do not meet the criteria, and thus almost all distributions from these investments are considered to be ordinary dividends.

Differentiating between ordinary and qualified dividends is not done at the ETF level but rather at the stock level. This means that a dividend received from one ETF can include some ordinary income and some qualified income, since some stock dividends paid to the ETF are themselves qualified while other stock dividends are not. This situation is more common in highly diversified ETFs. Rest assured, however, as your 1099 form will provide a breakout between ordinary and qualified dividends. Keep in mind that these tax rules—initially introduced in 2003—do have a termination date unless they are extended by Congress.

International (Common) Stock ETFs

U.S. companies are not the only companies throughout the global marketplace that pay stock dividends to their shareholders. Therefore, for ETFs that track international indexes, taking receipt of dividends paid by foreign companies is commonplace and so too are the taxes imposed by foreign governments on the money distributed. Foreign tax is paid by the ETF on behalf of its shareholders who in turn receive a 1099 form that shows both the dividend income received from foreign companies and the taxes paid by the ETF on their behalf. Shareholders are typically eligible for tax credits on their U.S. taxes for the foreign taxes paid during the same tax year.

U.S. Fixed-Income ETFs

Although the tax treatment for interest distributed from U.S. bonds is rather straightforward, there are some notable differences (i.e., exemption of interest and dividend yield) depending on the type of underlying bonds. As with investing in municipal bonds directly, the interest received from municipal bond ETFs is tax-exempt on the federal level, which is the most important tax to minimize, given its higher tax rate. If you invest in a national municipal bond ETF, then the interest will generally be taxable on the state level. However, there are single-state ETFs in existence that allow investors to avoid both the federal and state taxes on interest income. Most municipal bond ETFs hold bonds that are exempt from the federal alternative minimum tax (AMT).

Interest income from ETFs that hold U.S. government Treasury securities—such as the iShares Barclays 1–3 Year Treasury Bond (symbol: SHY)—are typically exempt from state and local taxes but are fully taxable on the federal level. As mentioned in Chapter 3, the yields on Treasury-linked ETFs will be lower than the yields on municipal-linked ETFs, but they will provide much higher safety of principal.

Corporate bond ETFs are fully taxable on all levels—federal, state, and local. However, the advantage of corporate bonds is higher net yields than most other bond yields. Interest income received from a corporate bond ETF is considered ordinary income and thus taxed at the shareholders highest income tax bracket.

Lastly, there's a new type of bond called a Build America Bond (BAB), which is issued by state and local governments; its interest payments may be subsidized by the U.S. Treasury. The subsidy allows issuers to pay higher rates of interest in order to compete against higher-yielding corporate bonds. These higher-yielding BABs are fully taxable on the federal level and are prized by tax-exempt investors. Another type of BAB provides bondholders with a tax credit from the federal government equal to 35 percent of the interest paid by the bond. The PowerShares Build America Bond (symbol: BAB) debuted in 2009 to capitalize on this new type of bond.

Preferred Stock ETFs

Income distributions from preferred stock ETFs are treated the same as distributions for equity (common) stock ETFs. The three largest preferred stock ETFs are iShares S&P U.S. Preferred Stock Index (symbol: PFF), PowerShares Financial Preferred (symbol: PGF), and PowerShares Preferred (symbol: PGX); each of the three has assets under management of over $1 billion. The primary reasons for investing in preferred stock ETFs are that the shareholder receives a higher-yielding dividend than he or she would get with common stocks, there's a modest price appreciation potential in some markets, and it's yet another way to enhance an asset allocation.

International Fixed-Income ETFs

As with U.S. fixed-income ETFs, international fixed-income ETFs pay interest income that is fully taxable under the IRS tax code. However, some interest income might be subject to foreign income taxes from the country of domicile of the issuing entity. Depending on the country and the tax treaty in place, the foreign tax withheld from investors may be eligible for a tax credit on U.S. taxes. Some of the interest income may be eligible for the credit; some may not. Each ETF will provide an end-of-year tax statement that outlines the sources of foreign income and the foreign tax credit eligibility. Given the heightened complexity of international fixed-income ETF tax treatment, it's advisable to seek the assistance of a tax professional when investing in this type of ETF.

Exchange-Traded Notes

Since many of the "ETFs" investors purchase are actually exchange-traded notes, or ETNs, an individual breakdown of their tax nuances is warranted. ETNs offer a highly tax-efficient way to invest, because equity-linked ETNs are treated as prepaid contracts (much like forward contracts) for tax purposes. More specifically, the buyer of a prepaid contract (i.e., the ETN) invests an initial amount in order to receive a future payment based on the value of an index or other underlying benchmark at a specified future date. In layperson speak: There is no distribution of dividends or interest—and resulting tax liability—with equity ETNs. In recent years there has been an increased scrutiny of the tax laws regarding ETNs. Currency and MLP (master limited partnership) ETNs are treated differently from equity ETNs. (See the "Currency ETFs" section for more specifics.) As for MLP ETNs, shareholders do receive quarterly distributions, and gains and losses from the partnerships are passed through to the individual investor; therefore, taxes accrue at the shareholder's level rather than at the fund level. Investors of MLPs typically receive a K–1 tax form instead of a 1099 for reporting a pro rata share of partnership gains and losses to the IRS. This form can be a headache for investors since not only is it another tax form to account for and file, but also it is typically distributed later in the tax season than is a 1099. Obviously tax-deferred and tax-exempt accounts do not have to worry about K–1s or 1099s.

Precious Metals ETFs

The tax treatment for investing in precious metals is not necessarily as cut-and-dried as it might initially appear, since it depends on how you gain your exposure to gold and silver, the two most popular precious metals. If you purchased an exchange-traded note, which is a debt instrument, then the tax treatment of any gains is the same as with any other ETN. Likewise, if you purchased a precious metals ETF that gains its exposure from futures contracts, then the tax treatment of any gains is the same as with any other ETF that holds futures contracts (see "Futures Contracts ETFs").

If, on the other hand, you purchased a precious metals ETF in which the ETF gains its exposure through the physical purchase and storage of actual bullion, then gains are subject to IRS tax treatment for "collectibles" such as art, jewelry, antiques, or coins. The current IRS code taxes gains for collectibles held for more than one year at a maximum rate of 28 percent, which is higher than the traditional capital gains tax rate. If your gain is considered to be short term (i.e., held for less than one year), then the maximum rate is generally the same as the shareholder's income tax rate.

Futures Contracts ETFs

ETFs that gain their exposure to commodities through futures contracts come with three unusual tax nuances. First, futures contracts are valued and taxed according to what is called "mark-to-market." For investors in futures-linked ETFs, this means that any open positions (held on the fund level) at the end of the tax year are treated as if they were sold at the close of trading at their final fair market value. Any resulting mark-to-market gains or losses are referred to as "deemed sales." Thus, the total capital gain (or loss) tax liability is the sum of any net gains from deemed sales plus net gains from actual sales made during the same taxable year.

Second, since most futures-linked funds are organized as master limited partnerships, shareholders will receive a K–1 tax form showing a pro rata share of the tax liability passed through by the fund to all shareholders.

Finally, pass-through shareholder gains and losses are taxed at the ratio of 60 percent long-term capital gains to 40 percent short-term capital gains, irrespective of the capital gains coming from actual sales or deemed sales. Since the tax rate on short-term capital gains is higher than the tax rate on long-term capital gains, this 60/40 tax split is disadvantageous to investors who hold their ETF for longer than one year; they would otherwise be subject to all long-term capital gains.

If the distribution of a K–1 and 60/40 tax split is not alluring to you, then consider a commodity-linked ETN instead. The difference in tax rules might make more sense to you.

Currency ETFs

As with other ETFs that track real asset indexes, currency-linked ETFs present their own unique tax treatment rules. The first nuance with currency-linked ETFs is that all long-term and short-term capital gains—as well as any monthly income distributions—are considered ordinary income under the IRS tax code. In addition, even if a fund that is legally structured as an ETN tracks currencies, then the tax treatment is the same as for currency-linked ETFs rather than for ETNs. Some currency-linked ETFs hold swaps and forward currency contracts, which can make some funds eligible for the 60/40 split between long-term and short-term capital gains; however, they must also use mark-to-market valuation, and thus they generate deemed sales gains. Finally, some shareholders of currency-linked ETFs will receive a K–1 tax form instead of a 1099.

As a result of the various differences among currency-linked ETFs, investigate each fund thoroughly and know the tax ramifications before you make the investment in a fully taxable account.

Leveraged and Inverse ETFs

Generally speaking, leveraged and inverse ETFs are less tax efficient than their nonleveraged and inverse counterparts on the traditional ETF side. As detailed in Chapter 3, leveraged and inverse ETFs invest in derivatives such as swaps, futures, and forwards in an effort to achieve their goal of either magnifying the performance of the tracking index or generating mirror opposite results of the tracking index— or both, in the case of leveraged inverse ETFs such as the Direxion Daily Financial Bear 3X Shares (symbol: FAZ).

Because these types of ETFs were engineered and are managed with the speculative trader in mind, turnover of the underlying derivative holdings will be higher than with other ETFs. The higher turnover will at times cause the ETF provider to liquidate underlying holdings, thus opening the ETF to short-term and/or long-term capital gains tax consequences. Any capital gains tax consequences are passed through to the shareholders and therefore generate a tax liability.

Some leveraged and inverse ETFs track commodities and currencies, so the tax consequences for these types of ETFs will match those of unleveraged and noninverse commodities and currency ETFs. In the case of precious metals ETFs, all gains will be taxed according to the 60/40 split and recorded and distributed on a K–1 tax form.

And lastly, since up to 90 percent of the underlying holdings of leveraged and inverse ETFs is invested in traditional securities, any dividend or interest payment made to the ETF can be passed through to the shareholder, thus creating an income tax liability.

CHAPTER 11

Keys for Winning with ETFs

Throughout this book you have found random keys on how to design, build, and manage an ETF portfolio for long-term success. This chapter presents the previously mentioned keys and introduces a few new ones. Many of these keys are commonsense ones, but some will be completely unknown to investors. Before beginning your endeavor into ETF investing, read through the following keys and try to use as many as possible. Note that the keys are not sorted in any particular order.

SCREEN OTHER CRITERIA FIRST, THEN INVESTIGATE HISTORICAL PERFORMANCE

We have all read and heard the disclaimer many times: past performance is not an indicator of future performance. This is pure common sense. So, if this statement is true, then why screen and evaluate performance at the beginning? Obviously, you should investigate historical performance to give you a hint of future potential, but that should be done at the end after you have screened for other criteria. Focus your time, energy, and resources on those criteria that are known and certain rather than those left to chance (i.e., performance).

Once you have completed your screening for other criteria, then evaluate historical performance to further refine your search for the ideal ETF. Remember that few ETFs will have a long track record, since so many ETFs have been launched within the last couple of years. If you are able to find solid, long-term historical performance, then screen for it. Immediately throw out those ETFs in the lowest fourth quartile and continue screening and comparing against the remaining peer-group ETFs under consideration.

SCREEN ETFs, AND AVOID OVERLAP

Not all ETFs, ETF providers, and indexes are created equal; there can be sizable differences. Be mindful of what's within each ETF, and screen each one as best as you can. For example, even though an ETF might have a generic name that indicates it has a value-oriented strategy, it may be more of a stealth financials ETF. That might mean unwanted overlap. Perhaps, too, you don't like financials and want to keep the exposure to a minimum, so this ETF might be inappropriate. Furthermore, a broad-based commodities ETF may in fact be a stealth energy ETF, given its substantial overweight to crude oil, natural gas, and heating oil and underweight to all nonenergy commodity classes. As a result, be careful when designing your asset allocation, as combining different categories of ETFs can lead to overlap. For instance, including an S&P 500 ETF and a technology-sector ETF in your portfolio will result in about 18 percent overlap. Including an energy-sector ETF in the same portfolio will generate another 12 percent overlap—in energy. If increasing the exposure to certain economic sectors is the goal, then there is no need to worry about the overlap. However, if inadvertently creating excessive exposure to any asset class, economic sector, or market segment is not desired, then be cautious of the ETFs you select to minimize any overlap in your portfolio.

For more sophisticated investors, drill down even more to understand the index the ETF tracks. Find out if the index is market based or custom based. Identify whether or not the index uses a market-weight approach or perhaps an equal-weight approach. The keys in this chapter provide many other ways to evaluate an ETE, but the point is to create a standardized process that you employ consistently. Remember the expression "garbage in, garbage out." Make sure your portfolio is not filled with garbage.

INDEX IT!

It's no secret that the majority of portfolio managers do not beat the return of their respective benchmarks in any given year. Furthermore, those portfolio managers who do get lucky enough to beat their benchmark have a lower probability of beating the market in the subsequent year. To top it off, active managers charge higher expense ratios to pay for their work and are more susceptible to conflicts of interest. On the other hand, ETFs that track market indexes not only offer a low-cost approach for building your optimal portfolio but also do so in a quick, easy, and efficient manner.

ETFs that track market indexes rather than custom indexes or strategies do not employ security selection or market timing to guide their investment choices. These ETFs are considered passive investments and managed in such a way as to match their return to that of a specific underlying index such as the S&P 500. ETFs that track market indexes have lower expense ratios, are more tax-efficient, offer consistent management, and provide greater transparency.

STICK TO FAMILIAR ETFs

The introduction of ETFs opened the doors to investing in complex securities and investing strategies that were never previously available, for all practical purposes, to casual investors. Prior to the advent of ETFs, most of these complex securities and investing strategies were the primary domain of professional investors and institutions. ETFs changed that arrangement by providing access to high-level investing opportunities for which some investors might not be ready or be a good match. For instance, commodity ETFs are typically the only way casual investors can gain exposure to certain commodity classes without trading futures contracts or buying the stocks of companies involved in the commodity space—and consequently being exposed to individual company problems. Having more options is typically better than not having them.

However, just because an investment is available now doesn't mean everybody should jump on it. Investors need to be keenly aware of what they are buying and how those things are impacting their portfolios. Going full speed ahead without knowing and understanding the risks and pitfalls can lead to the assumption of unintended risks in portfolios, which may not be consistent with investors' financial objectives and their risk-tolerance thresholds. Ultimately, it can result in a portfolio sinking—much like what happened to the *Titanic*.

Remember, ETFs can open doors, but you should walk through them only if you are familiar and comfortable with what's on the other side.

MINIMIZE USE OF LEVERAGED AND INVERSE ETFs

According to the SEC, leveraged and inverse ETFs are speculative investments and should only be employed by experienced, high-risk day traders. The SEC does not leave the door open even a crack for non–day traders such as you and I to purchase these types of ETFs. The SEC and some brokerage firms feel very strongly about this position, as accountability for purchase of these ETFs has shifted from the investor to the brokerage firm. Ambulance-chasing attorneys know this, and they are now stalking investors who have lost even a modest amount of money from these types of ETFs. Personally, I do not think all leveraged and inverse ETFs are speculative—it really depends on how you employ them. Inverse ETFs, when combined with a well-allocated portfolio, can provide a degree of hedging to safeguard against falling equity prices. However, the SEC is spot on when it claims that only experienced investors should consider employing leveraged and inverse ETFs. Novice and intermediate investors should steer clear of these higher (if not *ultra*-higher) risk investments.

INVEST DURING OPPORTUNE HOURS

One of the most compelling advantages of ETFs is their inherent stocklike tradability. This means that ETFs trade when stocks trade: between 9:30 a.m. and 4 p.m. Eastern Time. However, not all hours during the trading session are the same; there are more opportune times for placing ETF orders in certain types of ETFs over other times during the session (see Figure 11-1). The primary reason for the existence of opportune trading hours is related to when ETFs are valued, typically based on the portfolio composite file, which is calculated on the previous trading day. For instance, the best types of ETFs to trade when the market opens

Figure 11-1 **Opportune Hours for Investing**

include bonds (Treasuries and high yield) and international equities (European and Asian). Included in the early-morning equities are U.S. markets and emerging markets. U.S. markets are always opportune to trade, since the holdings in these ETFs include U.S. common stocks, which are traded continuously throughout each trading session. This lends itself to price discovery and low risk for lead market makers.

As the trading session progresses, ETFs that track European and Asian markets become less opportune to trade, since European markets close at 11 a.m. Eastern Time. Emerging markets and high-yield ETFs lose luster later in the trading day as well, but they retain some degree of idealness. As the trading session nears the closing bell, ETFs that track energies (specifically, crude oil) and metals begin to become more opportune. They do so because the futures markets close later in the day, which affords more robust market valuations from price discovery.

USE LIMIT ORDERS TO YOUR ADVANTAGE

The stocklike tradability of ETFs affords investors the opportunity to enter purchases and sales with multiple discretionary order types. One of the most impactful is the use of limit orders. When you place a market order, you will get the best market price for that ETF. But that does not mean that you cannot get a slightly better price with a limit order instead. With a limit order, you may not get your order filled immediately, but the extra wait time could save you from overpaying and thus keep your costs down. The best market price you see is but one indication of supply and demand for the ETF. By placing a limit order, you are telling the lead market maker what price you are willing to pay. This can result in a good fill, since the lots offered for sale can be at more favorable prices. Obviously, it does not make sense to place a limit order price significantly below the current best asking price, so be smart about where you place your orders.

SHOP FOR COMMISSION-FREE ETF ORDER EXECUTIONS

Minimizing all costs regardless of source is absolutely paramount to maximizing long-term performance. Small premiums and extra fees—as insignificant as they might appear when charged each year—can add up to a sizable amount over time. Before 2010, nearly all ETF purchase and sale order executions were assessed a trading commission, some small and some large, depending on the type of brokerage firm and platform employed. Given the increased competition for assets and clients, some of the leading discount brokerage firms began offering commission-free trading in select ETFs. Because of that, you ought to take a look at each brokerage firm's list of ETFs available for commission-free trading; if a firm's list is ideal for the type of ETFs you prefer, then give that firm serious consideration for custodying your account there. With commission-free order executions, you can still get the same ETFs you were going to purchase anyway but forgo the $8-per-trade commissions; if you make two trades per month, you can save nearly $200 per year in commissions.

CONSIDER SWAPPING ETFs FOR TAX-ADVANTAGED PURPOSES

If you hold a tax-deferred retirement account such as an IRA or a 401(k), then there is no need to worry about built-up unrealized capital gains and losses. However, if you invest in ETFs through a fully taxable investment account, then you need to keep a keen eye on both your realized and unrealized capital gains and losses. Depending on the situation, you may have opportunities to either minimize capital gains or use capital losses to your advantage when filing your taxes. For example, if you have no realized capital gains or losses and the end of the year is drawing near, then you can sell an ETF with built-up losses and use the proceeds to buy a similar, but not a near identical, ETF. You accomplish two things with this type of strategy. First, when you sell the ETF with an unrealized loss, you can use $3,000 of the loss as a deduction against your ordinary income when you file your taxes. Additional capital losses will be pushed forward to future tax years, so there is no worry about losing them. Second, when you sell and buy similar ETFs, you retain the asset allocation in your portfolio. That's very important, as investing considerations take a higher precedence over tax considerations. Note that eventually you will have to pay taxes on any capital gains generated with the purchased ETF, but you can defer that tax until the ETF is sold, which can be many years down the road. You can use the aforementioned strategy to minimize realized capital gains as well.

ALL ELSE BEING EQUAL, PICK LARGER ETFs OVER SMALLER ETFs

If you have the option of selecting a larger ETF to build out your asset allocation, then go with that ETF instead of a comparable smaller ETF. Obviously, if the smaller ETF fits a need that cannot be delivered by a larger one, then that warrants buying the smaller ETF. The reason for avoiding the smaller ETFs is not because of liquidity and average daily trading volume. The number of shares traded each day is not an indication of an ETF's liquidity; rather, liquidity is determined by the average liquidity of the underlying holdings. The reason for avoiding smaller ETFs is based purely on size and related concerns about the longevity of the fund. Each ETF has a certain degree of fixed costs that must be covered by the fund's expense ratio, which itself is based on the level of assets under management. Small ETFs have a difficult time operating efficiently and stand a much higher chance than large ETFs of being closed down by the ETF provider for lack of assets under management. Focus on ETFs with a minimum economical size of at least $10 million; better yet, choose one of $25 million or more.

BE CAUTIOUS WITH MEGA-SIZED ACTIVELY MANAGED ETFs

One of the drawbacks to investing in mega-sized actively managed mutual funds is the problem of the fund having too much money and not being able to invest it as desired. Over time as more and more investors commit money to a particular mutual fund, the fund becomes too big to generate the returns it had earned when it was smaller and more nimble and could take advantage of investable opportunities with relative ease. One of the best examples of this dilemma is the Magellan Fund from Fidelity Investments. Managed by legendary money manager Peter Lynch, this fund generated strong performance when fund assets were at a manageable level. Once investors began to recognize the strong returns the fund was generating, they began to invest in Magellan at increasing rates to get in on the action. Many financial experts say these capital inflows were too much for the fund to handle and thus the returns the investors were accustomed to earning were no longer being generated. Why does this occur? The reason is that funds get too large and cannot put the money to work in the same manner or under the same strategy they had traditionally used. That is not to say that the opportunities themselves disappear completely, only that the opportunities are only so large and even a modest investment from a titanic fund will exploit that opportunity fully.

To date, there is not a great concern over large actively managed ETFs because they have not developed that far yet—but some day it could become a real possibility. Remember what happened with the Magellan mutual fund, and be cautious with a mega-sized actively managed ETF.

BE ON THE LOOKOUT FOR NEW AND BETTER ETFs

ETFs have grown by over 1,000 percent during the 10-year period from 2001 to 2010. At the beginning of 2001 there were nearly 90 ETFs; by the end of 2010 there were almost 1,100 in total. If you started investing in ETFs in 2001 or 2002 and never changed the ETFs in your portfolio, then you missed over 1,000 new ETFs that could have enhanced your portfolio. Over the coming years, more and more ETFs will be launched, some good and some not so good. Since the industry is trending toward ever-lower fund costs as ETF providers look to have an advantage over the competition, you are bound to find an ETF comparable to one presently in your portfolio that has a lower expense ratio. Making a swap in this situation might be prudent, depending on the trading costs and any tax liability you might incur as a consequence. In addition to engineering better ETFs, providers strive for a first-mover advantage by adding new and different ETFs to their lineups of funds to capture more assets under management. In rare circumstances you might find a new and different ETF that should be inserted into your portfolio to either increase yield or enhance your asset allocation, thus ultimately reducing risk. In summary, stay on top of the ETF marketplace and be on the lookout for new or better ETFs.

ETF Resources

Books

Abner, David J., *The ETF Handbook*, Hoboken, New Jersey: John Wiley & Sons, 2010.

Appel, Marvin, *Investing with Exchange-Traded Funds Made Easy*, Upper Saddle River, New Jersey: FT Press, 2008.

Carrel, Lawrence, *ETFs for the Long Run*, Hoboken, New Jersey: John Wiley & Sons, 2008.

Delfeld, Carlton T., *ETF Investing Around the World*, Lincoln, Nebraska: iUniverse, 2007.

Dion, Don, and Carolyn Dion, *The Ultimate Guide to Trading ETFs*, Hoboken, New Jersey: John Wiley & Sons, 2010.

Ferri, Richard, *The ETF Book*, Hoboken, New Jersey: John Wiley & Sons, 2009.

Frush, Scott Paul, *All About Exchange-Traded Funds*, New York: McGraw-Hill, 2011.

Gastineau, Gary L., *The Exchange-Traded Funds Manual*, Hoboken, New Jersey: John Wiley & Sons, 2010.

Groves, Francis, *Exchange-Traded Funds*, Hampshire, U.K.: Harriman House, 2011.

Lofton, Todd, *Getting Started in Exchange-Traded Funds*, Hoboken, New Jersey: John Wiley & Sons, 2007.

Maeda, Martha, *The Complete Guide to Investing in Exchange-Traded Funds*, Ocala, Florida: Atlantic Publishing Group, 2009.

Meziani, A. Seddik, *Exchange-Traded Funds as an Investment Option*, Hampshire, U.K.: Palgrave Macmillan, 2005.

Richards, Jr., Archie M., *Understanding Exchange-Traded Funds*, New York: McGraw-Hill, 2007.

Vomund, David, and Linda Bradford Raschke, *ETF Trading Strategies Revealed*, Columbia, Maryland: Marketplace Books, 2006.

Wiandt, Jim, *Exchange-Traded Funds*, Hoboken, New Jersey: John Wiley & Sons, 2001.

Wild, Russell, *Exchange-Traded Funds for Dummies*, Hoboken, New Jersey: John Wiley & Sons, 2006.

Web Resources

Bloomberg: www.Bloomberg.com
CNBC: www.CNBC.com
CNN: www.CNNfn.com
ETF Guide: www.ETFGuide.com
ETF Market Watch: www.ETFMarketWatch.com
ETF Trends: www.ETFTrends.com
ETF Zone: www.ETFZone.com
Index Investor: www.IndexInvestor.com
Index Universe: www.IndexUniverse.com
Market Watch: www.MarketWatch.com
Morningstar: www.Morningstar.com
Motley Fool: www.Fool.com
MSN: MoneyCentral.MSN.com

Seeking Alpha: www.SeekingAlpha.com
The Street: www.TheStreet.com
Wall Street Journal: www.WSJ.com
Yahoo! Finance: Finance.Yahoo.com/ETF

ETF Providers

BlackRock (iShares)
525 Washington Boulevard, Suite 1405
Jersey City, NJ 07310
800-iShares
www.iShares.com

Invesco PowerShares Capital Management
301 West Roosevelt Road
Wheaton, IL 60187
800–983–0903
www.PowerShares.com

Van Eck (MarketVectors)
335 Madison Avenue, 19th Floor
New York, NY 10017
800–544–4653
www.VanEck.com

ProFunds Group (ProShares)
7501 Wisconsin Avenue
Bethesda, MD 20814
866–776–5125
www.ProShares.com

Rydex-SGI (now a part of Guggenheim Partners, LLC)
P.O. Box 758567
Topeka, KS 66675–8567
800–820–0888
www.Rydex-SGI.com

State Street Global Advisors (SPDRs)
One Lincoln Street, State Street Financial Center
Boston, MA 02111–2900
617–786–3000
www.SSgA.com

The Vanguard Group
P.O. Box 1110
Valley Forge, PA 19482–1110
800–992–8327
www.Vanguard.com

WisdomTree Investments
380 Madison Avenue, 21st Floor
New York, NY 10017
866–909–9473
www.WisdomTree.com

Index Sponsors

Dow Jones Indexes
P.O. Box 300
Princeton, NJ 08543–0300
609–520–7249
www.DJIndexes.com

MSCI
One Chase Manhattan Plaza, 44th Floor
New York, NY 10005
888–588–4567
www.MSCI.com

Russell Investments
1301 Second Avenue, 18th Floor
Seattle, WA 98101
866–551–0617
www.Russell.com

Standard & Poor's
55 Water Street
New York, NY 10041
212–438–1000
www.StandardAndPoors.com

Wilshire Associates
1299 Ocean Avenue, Suite 700
Santa Monica, CA 90401
310–451–3051
www.Wilshire.com

Brokerage Firms

Charles Schwab: www.Schwab.com or 1–866–232–9890
Fidelity Investments: www.Fidelity.com or 1–800–343–3548
Scottrade: www.Scottrade.com or 1–800–619–7283
TD Ameritrade: www.TDAmeritrade.com or 1–800–454–9272
Vanguard Group: www.Vanguard.com or 1–800–319–4254

Stock Exchanges

American Stock Exchange
See New York Stock Exchange

CME Group
20 South Wacker
Chicago, IL 60606
312–930–1000
www.CMEGroup.com

The Nasdaq Stock Market
One Liberty Plaza
165 Broadway
New York, NY 10006
212–401–8700
www.NASDAQ.com

New York Stock Exchange (NYSE Euronext)
11 Wall Street
New York, NY 10005
212–656–3000
www.NYSE.com

Finding an Investment Professional

CFA Institute
560 Ray C. Hunt Drive
Charlottesville, VA 22903–2981
800–247–8132
www.CFAInstitute.org

CFP Board
1425 K Street, NW, Suite 500
Washington, DC 20005
800–487–1497
www.CFP.net

Financial Planning Association
4100 E. Mississippi Avenue, Suite 400
Denver, CO 80246–3053
800–322–4237
www.FPAnet.org

National Association of Personal Financial Advisors
3250 North Arlington Heights Road, Suite 109
Arlington Heights, IL 60004
847–483–5400
www.NAPFA.org

Regulatory Entities

Financial Industry Regulatory Authority (FINRA)
1735 K Street, NW
Washington, DC 20006
301–590–6500
www.Finra.org

National Futures Association
300 South Riverside Plaza, Suite 1800
Chicago, IL 60606–6615
312–781–1300
www.nfa.futures.org

U.S. Commodity Futures Trading Commission
Three Lafayette Centre
1155 21st Street, NW
Washington, DC 20581
202–418–5000
www.CFTC.gov

U.S. Securities and Exchange Commission
100 F Street, NE
Washington, DC 20549
202–942–8088
www.SEC.gov

Asset Allocator Questionnaire

Asset allocation is the strategy of dividing an investor's wealth among the different asset classes and asset subclasses to achieve the highest expected total rate of return for the given level of risk the investor is willing, able, and needs to assume. Empirical evidence has shown that how you allocate your wealth, rather than which securities you select or when you buy or sell, determines the majority of your investment performance over time.

The asset allocator questionnaire will help you determine your risk profile (i.e., your tolerance, capacity, and need for risk) and help identify your optimal asset allocation. This worksheet presents a number of questions and, based on your responses, will suggest one of five optimal asset allocations that may be the most appropriate for you. Each optimal asset allocation is designed to give you the highest expected total rate of return for the level of risk you are willing, able, and need to assume.

The optimal asset allocations should not be considered investment advice and should be considered within the context of all relevant investment strategies and when making investment decisions. Last, since your objectives and constraints may change over time, you may want to revisit this questionnaire annually.

1. **What is your investment goal?**
   a. To make a purchase or pay an expense within three years using a substantial portion of my portfolio
   b. To provide a source of current income (interest and dividends)
   c. To balance capital appreciation with current income
   d. To emphasize capital appreciation over current income
   e. To emphasize aggressive capital appreciation

2. **What is your age group?**
   a. Under 39
   b. 40–49
   c. 50–59
   d. 60–69
   e. 70 or over

3. **How much of your portfolio do you anticipate liquidating and using to make purchases within the next five years?**
   a. 0%
   b. Between 1% and 15%
   c. Between 15% and 25%
   d. Between 25% and 50%
   e. Between 50% and 100%

4. **Approximately what percentage of your total investment holdings does this portfolio represent?**
   a. Less than 25%
   b. Between 25% and 50%
   c. Between 50% and 75%
   d. Between 75% and 100%

5. **How secure are your future sources of income (employ-ment, investment, and retirement)?**
   a. Very secure
   b. Secure
   c. Balanced
   d. Unsecure
   e. Very unsecure

6. **How strongly do you prefer securities with lower market-value volatility and lower expected returns over securities with higher market-value volatility and higher expected returns?**
   a. Strongly prefer
   b. Prefer
   c. Indifferent
   d. Do not prefer
   e. Strongly do not prefer

7. **When the market is doing well, do you prefer to sell less-risky investments and buy more-risky investments with the proceeds?**
   a. Strongly prefer
   b. Prefer
   c. Indifferent
   d. Do not prefer
   e. Strongly do not prefer

8. **Figure B-1 illustrates potential gains and losses a portfolio may experience over the next five-year period. Select the potential gain or loss grouping most preferable to you.**

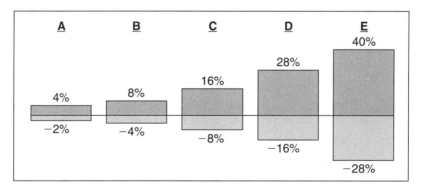

Figure B-1 **Hypothetical Range of Returns**

    a. Gains: 4%; losses: −2%
    b. Gains: 8%; losses: −4%
    c. Gains: 16%; losses: −8%

    d. Gains: 28%; losses: −16%

    e. Gains: 40%; losses: −28%

9. **About what percentage of your monthly net income is allocated to paying debt (not including your monthly mortgage payment on your principal residence)?**

    a. Between 0% and 15%

    b. Between 15% and 25%

    c. Between 25% and 50%

    d. Between 50% and 100%

10. **How many dependents do you financially support?**

    a. None

    b. Between one and three

    c. Four or more

11. **What is the size of your emergency fund?**

    a. I do not have one

    b. Between 1 and 3 months of average monthly expenses

    c. Between 4 and 6 months of average monthly expenses

    d. More than 6 months of average monthly expenses

12. **About what percentage of your retirement income do you anticipate coming from this portfolio?**

    a. Between 0% and 15%

    b. Between 15% and 25%

    c. Between 25% and 50%

    d. Between 50% and 100%

13. **What is your experience with equity investments?**

    a. Extensive experience

    b. Moderate experience

    c. Very little experience

    d. No experience

14. **What is your experience with fixed-income investments?**

    a. Extensive experience

    b. Moderate experience

c. Very little experience

d. No experience

15. **What is your experience with alternative investments (e.g., real estate, commodities, absolute return strategies)?**
    a. Extensive experience
    b. Moderate experience
    c. Very little experience
    d. No experience

16. **Please select ONE of the following that best describes your view of portfolio risk.**
    a. I prefer investments with low risk.
    b. I mostly prefer investments with low risk, but I am willing to accept some investments with moderate risk.
    c. I prefer a balanced approach of low-, moderate-, and high-risk investments.
    d. I mostly prefer investments with high risk, but am willing to accept some investments with moderate and low risk.
    e. I prefer investments with high risk.

17. **How much additional risk are you willing to assume to earn a higher expected total rate of return?**
    a. I am willing to accept more risk with all my investments to earn a higher expected total rate of return.
    b. I am willing to accept more risk with a portion of my investments to earn a higher expected total rate of return.
    c. I am willing to accept slightly more risk with all my investments to earn a higher expected total rate of return.
    d. I am willing to accept slightly more risk with a portion of my investments to earn a higher expected total rate of return.
    e. I am not willing to accept more risk to earn a higher expected total rate of return.

Score Section

For each number below, please circle the letter and corresponding score based on how you answered the preceding questions. The blank line at the end should be used to total your score.

1	[A] 1	[B] 3	[C] 6	[D] 9	[E] 12
2	[A] 12	[B] 9	[C] 6	[D] 3	[E] 1
3	[A] 12	[B] 9	[C] 6	[D] 3	[E] 1
4	[A] 10	[B] 8	[C] 6	[D] 4	
5	[A] 16	[B] 13	[C] 10	[D] 7	[E] 4
6	[A] 2	[B] 5	[C] 8	[D] 11	[E] 14
8	[A] 1	[B] 5	[C] 9	[D] 13	[E] 17
9	[A] 7	[B] 5	[C] 3	[D] 1	
10	[A] 5	[B] 4	[C] 3		
11	[A] 2	[B] 4	[C] 6	[D] 8	
12	[A] 8	[B] 6	[C] 4	[D] 2	
13	[A] 5	[B] 4	[C] 3	[D] 2	
14	[A] 5	[B] 4	[C] 3	[D] 2	
15	[A] 5	[B] 4	[C] 3	[D] 2	
16	[A] 1	[B] 5	[C] 9	[D] 13	[E] 17
17	[A] 13	[B] 10	[C] 7	[D] 4	[E] 1

Total Points = _____

33–58: If your score falls within the range of 33 to 58, you have a low-risk profile and should emphasize aggressive capital preservation.

59–84: If your score falls within the range of 59 to 84, you have a low- to moderate-risk profile and should emphasize capital preservation with some growth.

85–121: If your score falls within the range of 85 to 121, you have a moderate-risk profile and should emphasize a balanced approach to capital appreciation and capital preservation.

122–147: If your score falls within the range of 122 to 147, you have a moderate- to high-risk profile and should emphasize capital appreciation.

148–173: If your score falls within the range of 148 to 173, you have a high-risk profile and should emphasize aggressive capital appreciation.

Optimal Asset Allocations

The following are five optimal asset allocations that may be the most appropriate for you given the results of your answers. Each optimal asset allocation is designed to give you the highest expected total rate of return for the level of risk you are willing, able, and need to assume.

Scores Between 33 and 58: Aggressive Capital Preservation Portfolio
Equities: 25%
Fixed income: 55%
Cash and equivalents: 15%
Alternative assets: 5%

Scores Between 59 and 84: Capital Preservation Portfolio
Equities: 40%
Fixed income: 45%
Cash and equivalents: 10%
Alternative assets: 5%

Scores Between 85 and 121: Balanced Portfolio

Equities: 50%

Fixed income: 30%

Cash and equivalents: 10%

Alternative assets: 10%

Scores Between 122 and 147: Capital Appreciation Portfolio

Equities: 70%

Fixed income: 10%

Cash and equivalents: 5%

Alternative assets: 15%

Scores Between 148 and 173: Aggressive Capital Appreciation Portfolio

Equities: 70%

Fixed income: 5%

Cash and equivalents: 5%

Alternative assets: 20%

ETF Glossary

Accumulated dividends: Although only applicable to certain ETFs, *accumulated dividends* refer to the amount of cash an ETF has received and currently holds before cash dividends are issued to shareholders.

Actively managed ETF: An ETF (or mutual fund) that employs an active (as opposed to passive) investment strategy to meet its investment objective rather than tracking a market index. The investment strategy is based on a custom investment strategy and style of the ETF provider. Active management attempts to beat the market by employing security selection and market timing strategies.

Alpha: Risk-adjusted mathematical measurement of the so-called active return on an investment strategy calculated by subtracting the benchmark return from the actual return. The resulting figure is the return in excess of the compensation for the risk assumed.

Asset allocation: The strategy of dividing an investor's wealth among different asset classes and subclasses to achieve the highest expected total rate of return for that investor's tolerance, capacity, and need to assume risk.

Asset class: A group of securities that shares similar underlying characteristics as well as very similar risk and return trade-off profiles. The four primary asset classes are equities, fixed-income, cash and equivalents, and real assets. Each asset class can be further divided into asset subclasses, such as U.S. equities and international equities.

Authorized participants (APs): Also called "creation unit holders," authorized participants (APs) are typically large institutional investors, specialists, market makers, or lead market makers (LMMs) who have signed participant agreements with specific ETF providers to transact directly with providers in a process known as creations and redemptions.

Basis point: A measurement used primarily to quote bonds in which one basis point is equal to 0.01 percent, or one one-hundredth of 1 percent. For example, 100 basis points are equal to 1 percent, and 50 basis points are equal to 0.50 percent.

Benchmark: A yardstick or standard for measuring the performance of an investment. Most benchmarks are existing market indexes, such as the S&P 500 Index.

Beta: A volatility measurement for a security—such as an ETF or common stock—versus a comparable benchmark like the S&P 500 stock index. A security with a beta higher than the S&P 500 will rise or fall to a greater degree, and a security with a lower beta will rise or fall to a lesser degree.

Bid-ask spread: A spread that represents the difference between the purchase (or ask) price and the selling (bid or offer) price. One-half of the bid-ask spread is a cost to the buyer when an ETF is purchased, and one-half of the bid-ask spread is a cost to the seller when an ETF is sold. Liquidity is represented by the bid-ask spread.

Cash drag: The loss of potential performance as a result of an ETF not being fully invested. The vast majority of ETFs are fully invested because they do not have to satisfy shareholder withdrawal demands—a normal fact of life for mutual funds.

Closed-end funds: Like exchange-traded funds, closed-end funds are collective investments whereby investors pool their money in one fund that invests in an underlying basket of securities. Contrary to a misconception, closed-end funds are not closed to new investors; rather, closed-end funds do not issue new shares of the fund once the initial shares are sold to investors. Once that happens, the only way investors can purchase shares is in the secondary market on a stock exchange. This means that prices for closed-end funds are dictated by supply-and-demand forces, much like those of ETFs. However, closed-end funds do not involve authorized participants as ETFs do and therefore cannot arbitrage away any trading premiums or discounts to NAV.

Commission: The transaction fee paid to a broker for executing a securities trade. Commission amounts can vary and are often dictated by the number of shares, total trade value, the frequency of trades, and sometimes the size of the brokerage account.

Common stock: The most widely used form of equity ownership across the globe. Common stock shareholders have voting rights and often participate in receiving profits in the form of dividends. However, not all corporations distribute profits in the form of dividends. Rather, some reinvest the dividends back into their companies in order to fund existing operations and planned expenditures.

Correlation: The technical term used to measure from −1.0 to +1.0 how closely the market prices of two ETFs or other assets move together over time.

Creation unit: A large block of ETF shares—usually up to 50,000, but which can be as high as 600,000 and as low as 20,000—that comprise the underlying individual securities and estimated cash amount for each share of an ETF.

Custodian: An independent third-party financial institution that is responsible for holding and recording all of the securities and transactions occurring in an ETF. Custodians serve the traditional role of transfer agent and fund administrator.

Deferred sales charge: Also referred to as a "contingent deferred sales charge," or CDSC, a sales charge deducted from an investment fund for liquidating before a specific date or before the sales charge ceases to be applicable. The most prominent deferred sales charges are associated with mutual fund class B and C shares.

"Diamonds": The nickname for shares of the Dow Jones Industrial Average ETF—a unit investment trust—managed by State Street Global Advisors.

Diversification: A strategy designed to minimize investment-specific risk (thus reducing total risk) by combining a large number of securities within a particular asset class or market segment that exhibit similar risk and return trade-off profiles.

Dividend drag: The implicit cost some ETFs (unit investment trusts) incur as a result of SEC rules stipulating that these ETFs cannot reinvest dividends paid by securities held by the ETF back into the portfolio immediately. Instead, these ETFs must accumulate the dividends in a cash reserve account and pay them to shareholders at periodic intervals—typically quarterly. Open-end funds are not prohibited from reinvesting dividends back into the fund.

EAFE Index: Computed and published by MSCI, the EAFE Index is a market constructed index that tracks markets across Europe, Australia, and the Far East.

Efficient market hypothesis: This hypothesis states that market prices already reflect the full knowledge of investors, thus making it nearly impossible to outperform the market through stock picking or market timing. As an ultimate result, investors are discouraged from using fundamental research to find undervalued or mispriced securities.

Emerging markets: Economies or capital markets of developing countries that are often new, not fully established, or have a limited history and track record. Although there are over 150 countries meeting some classification standard of emerging market status, there are only about 40 officially recognized emerging markets in the world, with China and India the largest such markets.

Estimated cash amount: The estimated amount of cash per creation unit; it is designed to provide authorized participants with an idea of approximately how much cash per creation unit will be required to create or redeem ETF shares on a specific trading day.

Exchange-traded fund (ETF): An investment company organized under either the Securities Act of 1933 or the Investment Company Act of 1940 that has received certain exemptive relief from the SEC to allow secondary market trading in the ETF shares. ETFs offer shareholders, including those of moderate means, an opportunity to invest proportionately in a highly diversified, tax-efficient, and cost-effective basket of securities, such as common stocks, preferred stocks, bonds, real estate investment trusts (REITs), and commodities.

Exchange-traded note (ETN): First issued in 2006 by Barclays Bank, the exchange-traded note (ETN) is a debt instrument that tracks the return of a single currency, commodity, or index. In contrast to an exchange-traded fund, an ETN does not hold or represent a pool of underlying securities. Rather, an ETN is senior, unsecured, unsubordinated direct debt of a leading bank and registered under the Securities Act of 1933. ETNs employ an arbitrage strategy whereby market prices are closely linked to the intrinsic value of the benchmarks each ETN tracks. ETNs are established with 30-year maturities and offer no principal protection. In addition, they do not pay dividends or interest, do not offer voting rights to shareholders, and are subject to call provisions at the discretion of the issuer. The primary and totally unique drawback or risk of investing in an ETN is the credit risk associated with the issuing bank.

Exchange-traded portfolio (ETP): The term "exchange-traded portfolio" (ETP) is the more appropriate name for what we commonly refer to as exchange-traded fund. Since many special trusts, limited partnerships, and notes have the same look and feel as an ETF but do not possess many of the same important characteristics, the use of the name ETP in place of ETF is more descriptive and encompassing from a hierarchical perspective.

Exemptive relief: Acts taken by the SEC that allow ETFs to be exempt from certain provisions of the Investment Company Act of

1940. Without these exemptive relief actions, ETFs would not be possible.

Expense ratio: Expressed as a percentage of assets under management, an expense ratio represents the annual fee that an ETF charges its shareholders for such items as the management fee, trustee's fee, and license fee. This expense is an internal charge, but it is easily identifiable and totally transparent.

Financial Industry Regulatory Authority (FINRA): A self-regulatory organization (SRO) that oversees the market regulation of all securities firms doing business in the United States. FINRA was created in 2007 through the merger of the National Association of Securities Dealers (NASD) with the member regulation, enforcement, and arbitration divisions of the New York Stock Exchange (NYSE).

Free float: Float expresses the total number of shares publicly owned and "freely" available for trading. Free float is calculated by subtracting restricted shares from outstanding shares.

Fund flow: The inflow and outflow of invested money into or out of an ETF. Fund flow can be measured monthly, quarterly, and yearly.

Fund of funds: An investment strategy or actual security that seeks to diversify risk exposure and investment style among various investments. This type of fund invests in other stand-alone funds rather than in securities directly. The primary drawback is an extra layer of expenses.

Global ETF: An ETF that provides investment exposure to international developed and emerging markets as well as to the United States. This is a catch-all type of ETF that focuses almost exclusively on equities.

Gold ETF: A type of ETF designed to provide exposure to gold-related companies, commodity futures, or to physical gold itself. Gold companies can be engaged in the production, processing, or mining of gold whereas ETFs that track the price of gold itself will typically purchase and store physical gold or trade gold derivatives.

Grantor trust: An exchange-traded grantor trust is not an open-end investment company or a unit investment trust (UIT); instead, it is registered under the Securities Act of 1933. Shareholders have voting rights in the underlying company and can transact shares in round lots of 100. Dividends are not reinvested in the trust and are instead paid immediately to shareholders. The portfolio of stocks under the exchange-traded grantor trust does not change, and as a result it cannot be rebalanced. Over time, this arrangement will ultimately lead to a less diversified portfolio since some of the underlying stocks appreciate in value and percentage of total trust while others are removed because of merger, acquisition, or bankruptcy.

HOLDR (HOLding Company Depositary Receipt): A type of grantor trust, a HOLDR is managed by Merrill Lynch; each trust is initially organized with a basket of only 20 stocks with a narrow investment theme. Unlike other ETFs, a HOLDR does not have creation units and can only be bought and sold in 100-share increments. Shareholders may exchange 100 shares of a HOLDR for its underlying stocks at any time. Over time, the number of stocks in the trust can fall as the underlying companies are acquired or merge with other companies. Since no replacements are made to the trust, the ultimate result is a less-diversified investment over time.

Index: A statistical measure used to track the aggregate performance of stocks, bonds, commodities, and other markets or segments. Some of the most widely popular ones include the Dow Jones Industrial Average, S&P 500, and Nasdaq–100.

Index fund: A type of ETF (or mutual fund) that tracks the performance of a stock, bond, or commodity market index. Favored for its low fees and tax efficiency, an index fund is also referred to as a "passive fund." Market timing and security selection strategies are not employed with index investing.

International ETF: A type of ETF that provides investment exposure to the global portfolio outside the United States. Nearly all international ETFs are equity based.

Intraday indicative value (IIV): Also referred to as "intraday value" or "underlying trading value," this value is calculated and published under a separate symbol every 15 to 60 seconds. This calculation determines the most recent real-time market value of an ETF based on the market prices of the underlying securities plus any estimated cash amounts (accrued dividends) associated with the creation unit.

Inverse ETF: A type of ETF that seeks daily investment results, before fees and expenses, that correspond to $-1\times$ (or $-2\times$ to $-3\times$ for leveraged inverse ETFs) the daily performance of its underlying tracking index.

Investment Company Act of 1940: The "40 Act" regulates the organization of investment companies, including ETFs and mutual funds, that engage primarily in investing and trading in securities. The act requires investment companies to disclose their financial condition and investment policies to investors and to the general public on a regular and timely basis.

Investment grade: Investment grade is a broad rating referring to those issuers and/or individual bond issues deemed to be worthy of investment given their safety and ability to repay principal. Investment grade issuers and issues are given a rating of between Aaa and Baa3 from Moody's and AAA and BBB- from both Standard & Poor's and Fitch.

iShares: Legally structured as open-end mutual funds, iShares is the marketing name for the family of over 200 ETFs advised and marketed by BlackRock, the largest ETF provider.

Large cap: A large publicly traded corporation or large-cap stock with a market capitalization ("cap") in excess of $10 billion.

Lead market maker (LMM): Formerly known as a specialist, a lead market maker is a contracted liquidity provider on an exchange that is responsible for providing a continuous quote, managing the opening and closing auction, providing price discovery, and driving the inside quote a certain percentage of time throughout the day.

Leveraged ETF: A leveraged long ETF seeks daily investment results, before fees and expenses, that correspond to 2× to 3× the daily performance of its underlying tracking index. A leveraged inverse ETF seeks daily investment results, before fees and expenses, that correspond to –2× to –3× the daily performance of its underlying tracking index.

Liquidity: The ability to buy or sell an asset without substantially affecting the asset's price. In addition, liquidity refers to the relative ease with which an asset can be converted into cash upon sale. Liquidity is illustrated by a security's bid-ask spread.

Market capitalization: The total value of a publicly traded company. Market capitalization, or market cap, is calculated by multiplying the total number of shares outstanding by the market price per share.

Market price: The actual price as determined by supply and demand forces. Unlike traditional mutual funds, which are transacted at net asset value, the market price of an ETF may differ from the net asset value. Given the creation and redemption process, most ETFs typically trade at market prices very near their NAVs.

Market return: The total return of an ETF based on its market price at the beginning and end of the investment holding period. Market return can be different from the ETF's NAV return.

Micro cap: A very small-sized publicly traded corporation or micro-cap stock with a market capitalization typically between $10 million and $100 million.

Mid cap: A moderate-sized publicly traded corporation or middle-cap stock with a market capitalization typically between $1 billion and $10 billion.

Net asset value (NAV): The value of each share of an ETF as determined by the value of its underlying holdings, including cash. NAV is calculated by dividing the total net assets in an ETF by the number of outstanding shares.

Net asset value return: NAV return, which can be different from market return, is the total return of an ETF based on its net asset value at the beginning and end of the investment holding period. However, the market return—and not the NAV return—is the return actually earned by ETF shareholders.

Open-end fund: An open-end fund structure allows an ETF to employ index sampling and optimization and to reinvest immediately dividends received from companies held in the fund, both of which are in contrast to the unit investment trust structure. Reinvesting dividends reduces dividend drag and therefore tracking error.

Option: A class of derivative that derives its value from the worth of an underlying asset. An option gives the owner the right, but not the obligation, to purchase (a call option) or sell (a put option) an underlying asset at a specific price (i.e., a strike price) before a specified expiration date all for a market-determined cost (i.e., premium).

Portfolio composition file: Created by an ETF provider or trustee each day after the close of market, this file tells authorized participants the securities and number of shares as well as the estimated cash amount that are required to build a creation unit on the next trading day. This file is used to calculate the intraday indicative value (IIV) for the majority of ETFs.

Preferred stock: An equity class of ownership in a corporation that has a higher claim on the assets and earnings than does common stock. Generally without voting rights, preferred stock typically offers not only a higher-yielding dividend than common stock but also a higher priority on receiving that dividend before common stock dividends are paid.

Premium to NAV: A pricing discrepancy whereby the market price for an ETF is higher than its net asset value. The creation and redemption process was specifically designed to minimize the existence of premiums with ETF pricing.

Prospectus: Required by securities laws, a prospectus is the written legal document that is distributed by an investment management company for the purpose of disclosing a fund's investment objectives, operating history, fund management, management fees, portfolio holdings, and other related financial data.

Qubes: Derived from its ticker symbol "QQQ," Qubes is the nickname for the PowerShares Nasdaq–100 tracking ETF, one of the most heavily traded ETFs in the marketplace today.

Real estate investment trust (REIT): A trust that raises money from shareholders and invests the money in property and/or mortgages. Federal regulations stipulate that 95 percent of earnings must flow to shareholders. REITs offer increased ways to enhance asset allocation and pay higher dividend yields than other types of stock.

Regulated investment company (RIC): An investment company in which capital gains, dividends, and interest earned on underlying investments are passed through to shareholders. This is done in order to avoid double taxation at both the fund level and shareholder level; instead, it is subject to taxation only at the shareholder level.

Sector fund/ETF: A type of fund that invests exclusively in businesses that operate in one of the ten economic sectors of the economy. Since the holdings of this type of ETF are in the same grouping, there is an inherent lack of diversification—and thus higher risk—than with traditional broad-based ETFs as defined by size (large cap, mid cap, and small cap) and style (value and growth).

Securities Act of 1933: This act requires that any offer or sale of securities that uses the means and instrumentalities of interstate commerce be registered by filing a registration statement—typically along with a prospectus—with the SEC. The SEC then conducts a thorough screening of the proposed security—a process that can take many months or even years.

Shares outstanding: The number of shares an ETF has issued as of the close of the market on the previous trading day. This number, expressed in the thousands, is used to calculate net asset value and market capitalization, among other things.

Small cap: A small-sized publicly traded corporation or small-cap stock with a market capitalization typically between $100 million and $1 billion.

SPDRs: SPDRs, or "spiders," are a family of ETFs managed by State Street Global Advisors (SSgA) that tracks a variety of market indexes. The name is an acronym for the first member of the ETF family: the Standard & Poor's Depositary Receipts (symbol: SPY). SPDR is a trademark of Standard and Poor's Financial Services, a subsidiary of McGraw-Hill Companies.

Subsidy trading costs: Otherwise known as "flow costs," subsidy trading costs are expenses borne by mutual fund shareholders as a result of the mutual fund needing to liquidate holdings to satisfy shareholder liquidations. Existing shareholders pay for the transactions costs of a shareholder who leaves the fund.

Tickers: Tickers, or symbols, refer to the lettering system used to identify a single stock, mutual fund, or ETF on an exchange. Each ETF is assigned a ticker.

Tracking error: A ratio expressed as a percentage that measures the unplanned deviation of return generated by an ETF compared with the return of an index benchmark over a fixed period of time. Over time, the greater the use of passive management, the smaller the tracking error tends to be. Tracking error is expressed as either a positive number for outperformance of the ETF or a negative number for underperformance. Deviations between the returns are generally very small and thus expressed in basis points rather than full percentage points.

Transparency: Transparency refers to many characteristics of an ETF. It is most commonly associated with how the holdings of an ETF are fully disclosed daily after the close of trading on the listing exchange and prior to the opening of trading on the exchange the following day.

Unit investment trust (UIT): A type of legal structure many early ETFs, such as the Select Sector SPDRs, employed and continue to employ. Its two primary drawbacks include the lack of reinvesting dividends immediately from the underlying holdings and the need to replicate an index by including all index constituents by their weightings.

Volatility: A measure of the amount of risk or uncertainty regarding the size of changes in a security's value. Volatility is a statistical measure of the dispersion of returns for a given security or market index. Higher volatility translates into higher risk and lower volatility into lower risk.

Yield: The annual rate of return for an interest payment or dividend payment received. It is derived by dividing the total annual interest or dividend payments by the purchase price or market value (depending on when and how you are evaluating the security).

Index

The letter *f* following a page number indicates that a figure is present.

About the Author

Scott Paul Frush is a leading authority on asset allocation policy and portfolio optimization using exchange-traded funds. He has helped investors safeguard and grow their wealth for nearly two decades. Scott is founder of Michigan-based Frush Financial Group and publisher of the *ETF Market Watch* newsletter and blog (www.ETFMarketWatch.com).

Scott's professional hallmark is the engineering and sustainability of highly diversified, low-expense, tax-efficient ETF portfolios under an optimal asset allocation policy and a disciplined rebalancing strategy.

Scott earned a master of business administration degree from the University of Notre Dame and a bachelor of business administration degree in finance from Eastern Michigan University. He holds the Chartered Financial Analyst (CFA) and Certified Financial Planner (CFP) designations.

Scott is the author of six other investing books: *All About Exchange-Traded Funds* (McGraw-Hill, 2011), *Commodities Demystified* (McGraw-Hill, 2008), *Hedge Funds Demystified* (McGraw-Hill, 2007), *Understanding Hedge Funds* (McGraw-Hill, 2006), *Understanding Asset Allocation* (McGraw-Hill, 2006), and *Optimal Investing* (Marshall Rand Publishing, 2004).

In 2010, Detroit-based *DBusiness* magazine named Scott to its "Thirty in Their 30s" annual list in recognition of his professional achievements before the age of 40. In addition, Scott is the 2007 recipient of *CFA Magazine's* prestigious "Most Investor Oriented" award, which recognizes one CFA Institute member who has made outstanding contributions to investor education. In 2008 Scott was profiled in *Bank Investment Consultant* magazine; the article highlighted his expertise with exchange-traded fund portfolios.

The Frush Financial Group Web site is located at www.Frush.com.